Room for Romance

The Ultimate Guide to Romantic Hotels

Great Britain and Ireland

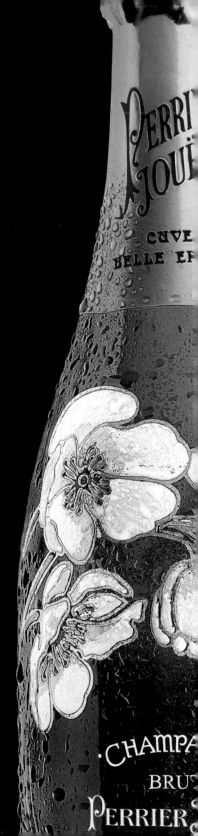

CHAMPAGNE
PERRIER JOUËT

Unforgettable.

Allied Domecq Spirits & Wine (UK) Ltd. Prewetts Mill, Worthing Road, Horsham, West Sussex, RH12 1ST

foreword

"Let's do it.
Let's fall in love"

Cole Porter

We're all romantics at heart – and that's why we think you'll love **Room for Romance**. If you're looking for somewhere special to take someone special, you'll find it here.

Other hotel guides do a fine job of grading properties according to strict (and predictable) criteria. We're happy to leave it to them. Our approach, we're glad to say, is subjective rather than formulaic.

Room for Romance brings together a collection of quintessentially romantic places to stay – places to fall in love with, and to fall in love in. We have chosen properties with those intangible qualities that make them heart-stealers perfect for a getaway à deux: rich in ambience and individuality, big on style, strong on history and passionate about great food and service.

The 90 hotels, inns, castles, manor houses and chic city bolt-holes (not forgetting a luxury ship and a train) featured within these pages are all romantic for different reasons. One may have fabulous views or gorgeous gardens; others may have seductive suites, stunning decor or dining to die for. Still more have hosts who have quite simply imbued their property with a supreme sense of specialness.

Whatever the qualities that lend them romantic appeal, all – from intimate inns to palatial estates – are the best of their kind. And none is the kind of place where you will be besieged by noisy children, droves of delegates or pre-packaged corporate greetings.

This is the first edition of **Room for Romance**, so do let us have your feedback – and of course your votes for our Hotel of the Year 2003. Turn to page 115 for more details and the chance to win a luxury weekend for two. In the meantime, read on. And enjoy!

Room for Romance

Editor	**Mike North**
Series editor	Marion Cotter
Designer	Wilcox Yap
Production editor	Kayla Hochfelder
Production co-ordinator	Lisa Penrose
Illustrations	Christine Coirault
	Wilcox Yap
Web design	Greg Stevens
Assisted by	Chris Shipton
Admin	Frieda Yeo
Sales	Nigel Bellwood
Managing editor, Freeway Media	Sophie Mackenzie
Hotel consultant	Michael Yeo
Publisher	Marion Cotter
Reproduction	Zebra, London
Printing	Mondadori, Spain
Distribution	Portfolio Books 020 8997 9000

First published in September 2002
Published by Freeway Media Ltd, 4 Ravey Street, London EC2A 4XX
T +44 (0)20 7739 1434   **F** +44 (0)20 7739 1424
info@room4romance.com   www.room4romance.com

ISBN 09-531746-4-6
Copyright © September 2002 Freeway Media Ltd

Contents

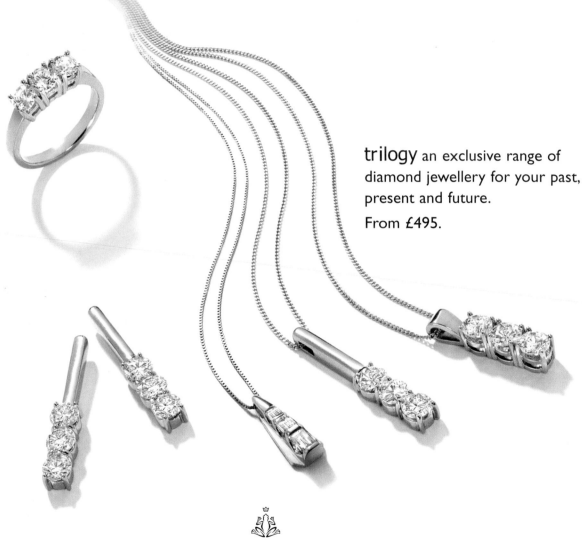

Practicalities

What makes a Room for Romance?

Whether they are grand moated manors or pint-size inns, all the places to stay featured here have been personally selected on the basis of their style, standards and romantic appeal. Our choice is not guided by the stars, accolades and facilities which preoccupy other guides, but by the location and loveliness of a property – a sense that its feel and philosophy make it tailor-made for celebrating, sharing special times and having fun together.

We hope – though of course we cannot guarantee – that you share our views. We also recognise that there may be other places which merit inclusion in our next edition, and warmly welcome readers' personal recommendations – all of which will be checked out. You can email us at info@room4romance.com.

Tariffs

The tariffs quoted on each page cover the cost of a standard double room for two people including full breakfast and VAT, unless otherwise stated. These costs were correct at the time of going to press, but are of course subject to change. They should therefore be taken as a guide rather than a price guarantee. Don't forget that most hotels offer special deals or short-break packages at different times of the year (especially if you're happy to travel midweek), so check out what's available when you book. There are often bargains to be had.

Some hotels may only accept two-night bookings at weekends, and most will expect a credit card guarantee when taking reservations. Do remember that cancellation charges normally apply. Almost all the properties featured in this guide accept payment by American Express and other major credit and debit cards. When making your reservation, don't forget to mention that you found the hotel in *Room for Romance*!

Eating and drinking

The dining experience is immensely important when it's just the two of you. While we leave it to other guides to grade hotels according to their formal culinary achievements, only those places which enjoy high standards of cooking are featured within these pages. A handful of our properties do not serve dinner in-house, but are generally well located for nearby restaurants,

❧ 9

Lovers' Lodge

and have proprietors who are only too happy to suggest a convivial or intimate place to dine. Many hotels have a dress code for dinner, so do check in advance.

Smoking

Note that smoking is sometimes not permitted in either bedrooms or dining areas, or both. If you are strongly anti (or pro) the weed, it's best to check out a hotel's policy before booking.

www.room4romance.com

Do visit our website at **www.room4romance.com**. You'll find a regularly updated bulletin board detailing news, late offers and special deals on accommodation, updates on forthcoming editions of *Room for Romance*, interactive maps and a picture of each property. Plus you'll be able to order further copies of this guide online, vote for our Hotel of the Year 2003, enter our prize draw to win a weekend at luxurious Stapleford Park (see page 115) and email us your views and feedback.

Symbols

The symbols shown with each page entry denote facilities either on the premises or nearby. Since a proprietor's view of what constitutes 'nearby' may differ from your own, do check first if a particular amenity – be it golf, tennis, swimming or a spa – is of special interest.

Note that the swimming symbol may denote an indoor or outdoor pool (the latter, of course, being seasonal), or in some cases, nearby beach swimming. The spa symbol may mean that treatments like massage or aromatherapy are available, or that the hotel has a sauna, solarium and fitness room. Again, we recommend that you check when booking to confirm exactly what is offered. The disabled friendly symbol denotes wheelchair access to at least one of the bedrooms, in addition to the hotel's public areas.

Key to symbols

 Four-poster beds
 Scenic setting
 Spa facilities
 Swimming
 Tennis
 Golfing
 Weddings held
Disabled friendly

Note: swimming, tennis, golf and spa facilities may be on the property or nearby.

Ullapool
11
13
4
Inverness
9
The Highlands
Aberdeen
1
7
5
Perth
10
Oban
2
Edinburgh
6 12 14
3
Glasgow
Ayr
8

Why we love Scotland

Its rugged beauty has inspired and captivated lovers from around the world

Glowing tartans and flickering firelight will keep you cuddling

After a couple of glasses of fine whisky, you can pretend to be the star-crossed lovers of *Braveheart*

When it rains, you've got the perfect excuse to hang up the Do Not Disturb sign

"Drink to me only with thine eyes,
And I will pledge with mine;
Or leave a kiss but in a cup
And I'll not look for wine."

Ben Jonson

Castleton House Hotel

By Glamis, Angus, DD8 1SJ
tel: 01307 840340
fax: 01307 840506
hotel@castletonglamis.co.uk
www.castletonglamis.co.uk

Rooms and rates
6 rooms.
Double room for 2 people
per night including full
breakfast and VAT from
£110 to £150

Proprietors
David Webster &
Verity Nicholson

The prettiest sight greets visitors to this part of Tayside. This fine house and its grounds, hidden by tall trees, are surrounded by the remains of a medieval moat. In season its steep banks are strewn with a variety of wild flowers (though its sylvan setting is lovely any time of year). An elderly and proud peacock claims this as his territory. The house has its own brilliant plumage – filled as it is with good antiques and decorative refinement. Within it the owners provide a warm and relaxing environment which, they hope, 'sets the mood for an exciting tryst.'

The Phew! factor

Follow the path of the moat under the rhododendron arch and along the bluebell banks.

Desirable Distractions Some of Angus's most impressive scenery: Glen Isla on one side, North Sea coast on the other. Glamis Castle, former home of the late Queen Mother, is close by. Visit Kirriemuir, home of *Peter Pan* author JM Barrie; and try another form of flying, falconry.

Love Bites Head chef Andrew Wilkie's award-winning fare and eclectic menus are sourced from the best of local ingredients and home-grown garden produce. Guests are urged not to hold back. Under-floor heating in the conservatory makes it an inviting place to dine whatever the weather.

Pillow Talk All eight bedrooms are traditionally decorated; in one there's an early Regency four-poster complete with feather duvet to sink into. Very Beau Brummel. You'll appreciate the many thoughtful extras such as a vase of fresh garden flowers.

Getting There Drive north along the A90 towards Forfar, then take the A928 to Glamis.

Cromlix House

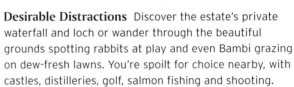

Kinbuck, Nr. Stirling
Perthshire FK15 9JT
tel: 01786 822125
fax: 01786 825450
reservations@cromlixhouse.com
www.cromlixhouse.com

Rooms and rates
14 rooms including 8 suites.
Double room for 2 people
per night including full
breakfast and VAT from
£205. Suites from £245.

Proprietors
David & Ailsa Assenti

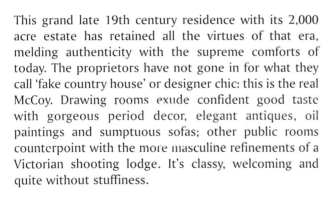

This grand late 19th century residence with its 2,000 acre estate has retained all the virtues of that era, melding authenticity with the supreme comforts of today. The proprietors have not gone in for what they call 'fake country house' or designer chic: this is the real McCoy. Drawing rooms exude confident good taste with gorgeous period decor, elegant antiques, oil paintings and sumptuous sofas; other public rooms counterpoint with the more masculine refinements of a Victorian shooting lodge. It's classy, welcoming and quite without stuffiness.

The Phew! factor

It has to be the private fairytale chapel – which might easily move you to tie the knot, or renew your vows.

Desirable Distractions Discover the estate's private waterfall and loch or wander through the beautiful grounds spotting rabbits at play and even Bambi grazing on dew-fresh lawns. You're spoilt for choice nearby, with castles, distilleries, golf, salmon fishing and shooting.

Love Bites There's a choice of candlelit dining rooms, each with open fires and its own charmingly distinct character, replete with the works: gleaming silverware, heavy crystal and fine china on crisp white linens. The award-winning menu and the wine list are corkers.

Pillow Talk The eight sumptuous suites are vast enough for some playful hide-and-seek before tumbling into the 6ft 6in canopied brass beds (too short for Liam Neeson, who caused a few flutters when he stayed here!). Hedonistic bathrooms have fluffy robes and luxury toiletries.

Getting There Cromlix House lies minutes off the A9, four miles north of Dunblane (Stirling). It is a 20 minute drive to Gleneagles and Perth, or 40 minutes to Glasgow.

Enmore Hotel

Hunters Quay, Dunoon
Argyll PA23 8HH
tel: 01369 702230
fax: 01369 702148
enmorehotel@btinternet.com
www.enmorehotel.co.uk

Rooms and rates
9 rooms including 2 suites.
Double room for 2 people
per night including full
breakfast and VAT from
£90 to £170

Proprietors
Angela & David Wilson

The Enmore Hotel, a mile north of Dunoon on the road to the Isles, was originally built in 1785 as a retreat for a wealthy Glasgow businessman named Wilson. Some 200 years on, his unrelated namesakes, Angela and David, have restored this pretty Georgian house into one of the most appealing and well-tended hotels on the Firth of Clyde, with brilliant west coast views, three comfortable lounges and a cocktail bar. The owners are sociable and solicitous. There are four honeymoon suites – some with a jacuzzi bath – with luxurious extra touches.

The Phew! factor

Snazzy jacuzzi and spa baths – some with underwater lighting. Mmm.

Desirable Distractions With Bute and Arran not far away, Dunoon is the gateway to the Western Isles. This charming town, with a boardwalk ideal for strolling, also has championship links. Then there are castles – Inverary, Dumbarton and Rothesay – and gardens nearby.

Love Bites David invests his menus with considerable invention and style. Diners choosing the baked Alaska are offered a keepsake photograph of themselves tucking in. Brilliant Aberdeen au jus steaks can be enjoyed here too.

Pillow Talk Nine luxurious, prettily decorated ensuite bedrooms, most with four-posters, half-testers, or a canopied bed. Fresh flowers, towelling robes and spa therapy products – even a pair of binoculars in suites with seaward views. If you're not otherwise engaged, focus them on the flower-filled gardens and beyond.

Getting There Travel from Glasgow on the M8/A8 through Greenock and Gourock and over on one of the two ferries or via Loch Lomond and the A815 to Dunoon.

Glenelg Inn

Glenelg Bay, Ross-shire
IV40 8JR
tel: 01599 522273
fax: 01599 522283
christophermain@glenelg-inn.com
www.glenelg-inn.com

Rooms and rates
6 rooms.
Double room for 2 people
per night including full
breakfast, dinner and VAT
from £158 to £198

Proprietor
Christopher Main

On one side the Isle of Skye: and facing it on the Scottish mainland is Glenelg Inn, gardens tumbling down to the sea and stunningly located, as befits its name, amongst glens. That's two for the price of one, so to speak. Actually, make that three – when you cross the threshold and enter the inn itself (named after a legendary Celtic hunting haunt). There's nothing mythical about owner Christopher Main's friendly welcome, nor the hospitable atmosphere that radiates in this characterful and traditionally furnished home from home.

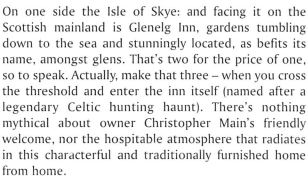

The Phew! factor

An impressive record of conception here – apparently due to the ley lines running through the village!

Desirable Distractions Explore the places that inspired Gavin Maxwell's classic *Ring of Bright Water*: by boat to lochs, tiny islands and hidden caves. There are historical reminders too: of Jacobite rebellion and the famed 2,000-year-old Pictish Broch Towers. And don't forget those glens: for wildlife, pony trekking, fishing and hill walking.

Love Bites Charming and intimate dining room where the good value menu utilises wholesome Scottish fare, with fish and seafood a speciality. How does fresh west coast monkfish, crisp fried, served on spiced couscous with salsa verde sound?

Pillow Talk Isle be seeing you – particularly since each of the six bedrooms has unrestricted views of Skye. Deeply comfortable and uncluttered surrounds; bathrooms whose soft peaty water apparently has recuperative powers.

Getting There From Inverness or Fort William take the A887/A87 to Shiel Bridge, turn left onto the country road and follow the signs to Glenelg Inn.

Hebridean Princess

Griffin House, Broughton Hall
Skipton, North Yorks BD23 3AN
Tel: 01756 704704
Fax: 01756 704794
reservations@hebridean.co.uk
www.hebridean.co.uk

Rooms and rates
30 cabins.
Double cabin for 2 people
per 7 night cruise
including all meals and
VAT from £2,830

Managing Director
Michael Fenton

Exploring the most wildly romantic shores of the British Isles aboard the sumptuous Hebridean Princess has to be the ultimate high. This cachet-laden cruiser – all teak decks and polished brass – noses through the Western Isles of Scotland and across the Irish Sea in enviable style. Days are spent discovering scenic spots in this rugged wildlife paradise often only accessible by boat (and teeming with puffins, seals and porpoises), while at night you'll drop anchor in some secluded bay. Passengers are fabulously spoilt by a crew whose sole aim is to please. Definitely fit for a Princess (and her prince).

The Phew! factor

While this high seas romance doesn't come cheap, it doesn't come finer.

Desirable Distractions Landing craft will whisk you ashore for an array of excursions on islands as varied as Rum, Skye, Harris, Iona and St Kilda. Pedal off on your own (the ship has its own bicycles), discover untrodden beaches or glimpse rare birdlife. Watch the sun sink over the Western Isles while you savour a pre-dinner whisky on deck.

Love Bites With some of Scotland's most talented young chefs on board, you're in for nightly epicurean treats – not to mention daytime picnics ashore. Dinner might feature pot roast quail carved over a truffle and garden herb risotto drenched with grapes and pine nuts in a shallot essence. Breakfasts are legendary. Peckish?

Pillow Talk Beautifully outfitted bedrooms are matched by marbled bathrooms. Slumber to the soporific sound of water lapping against the hull.

Getting There You'll be met at Glasgow Airport or rail station, before boarding the ship's specially chartered coach for the Argyll port of Oban.

The Howard

34 Great King Street
Edinburgh EH3 6QH
tel: 0131 557 3500
fax: 0131 557 6515
reserve@thehoward.com
www.thehoward.com

Rooms and rates
18 rooms.
Double room for 2 people
per night including Scottish
breakfast and VAT from
£275 to £395

General Manager
Johanne Falconer

Edinburgh is indisputably one of Britain's great cities, and its handsome Georgian architecture conjures up the best of that era. It's personified in this 1820's New Town building which combines three elegant townhouses. Gorgeous looking it most definitely is: you'll find a dramatic sweeping staircase, period murals, sash windows swathed in damask and brocades, fine antiques and oils in this five-star deluxe property. In short, The Howard exudes an air of aristocratic luxury and calm; the owners want visitors to feel like private guests in a miniature stately home. We think you will.

The Phew! factor

The suites demand luxuriating. So stay put and summon the butler to attend your every whim.

Desirable Distractions Stroll hand in hand down the Royal Mile, or do some window shopping in Princes Street. Don't forget historic Edinburgh – so off to the Castle, Holyroodhouse and the New Museum of Scotland.

Love Bites There's a choice of the formal dining room or in-room dining, where the cuisine is stylishly delivered by your dedicated butler. Starters might include tartlets of wild mushrooms and Dunsyre blue cheese; mains such as saffron spiced monkfish tail, then panna cotta with fruit and vanilla syrup to finish. And so to bed...

Pillow Talk Rooms have names not numbers, and some even boast their own street entrance. These are sumptuous spaces with high ceilings and large windows. Individual features are highlighted: choose Cockburn for views of the Firth of Forth, Abercromby for its generous four-poster, and Lauriston for its roll-top bath for two.

Getting There The Howard is a five minute taxi journey from Waverley station and eight miles from the airport.

Isle of Eriska

Ledaig, by Oban
Argyll PA37 1SD
tel: 01631 720371
fax: 01631 720531
office@eriska-hotel.co.uk
www.eriska-hotel.co.uk

Rooms and rates
17 rooms.
Double room for 2 people
per night including full
breakfast and VAT from
£225 to £270

Proprietor
Beppo Buchanan-Smith

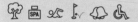

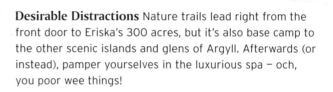

The bridge linking the west coast of Scotland to the tiny private island of Eriska is one well worth taking. Here's a romance-steeped hideaway that's both peaceful and remote: an impressive castellated house whose flowered lawns stretch down to woods teeming with wildlife; meadows where Highland cattle graze, banks where badgers nest (watch them come down to the library steps for their supper!) and Atlantic waters where grey seals frolic. The baronial comforts of the hotel, with its roaring log fires, West Highland welcome (even more warming) and attentive service extends the island magic.

The Phew! factor

Stroll along Eriska's deserted shores while watching the sun sink over the Western Isles.

Desirable Distractions Nature trails lead right from the front door to Eriska's 300 acres, but it's also base camp to the other scenic islands and glens of Argyll. Afterwards (or instead), pamper yourselves in the luxurious spa – och, you poor wee things!

Love Bites The catch of the day has been trawled in just hours earlier; juicy mushrooms were picked at dawn; wild salmon is fresh from the loch; beef is some of Scotland's finest. Vegetables and herbs, home grown, zing with flavour. A pretty good start, that.

Pillow Talk Rooms are beautifully appointed, with sumptuous beds and bathrooms. Lock yourselves in the tower; ideally in the Glesanda Room, with its to-die-for views across the Firth of Lorne. Eriska's Colonsay and Mull rooms have great outlooks, too.

Getting There Take the A82 north, then follow the A85 towards Oban. At Connel proceed by bridge to the village of Benderloch. Eriska is well signposted from there.

Knockinaam Lodge

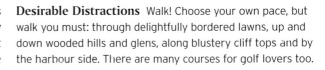

Portpatrick, Dumfries & Galloway DG9 9AD
tel: 01776 810471
fax: 01776 810435
reservations@knockinaamlodge.com
www.room4romance.com

Rooms and rates
10 rooms. Double room for 2 people per night including full breakfast and VAT from £180 to £340

Proprietors
Michael Bricker & Pauline Ashworth

Even with a wind blowing there's a wonderful stillness around this remote and undeniably romantic hideaway surrounded on three sides by cliffs and looking out across pretty gardens towards the Irish Sea. Intimate public rooms are traditionally furnished in pastels that enhance the feeling of tranquillity. There's often a log fire crackling, and its gentle heat seems to deepen the scent of fresh lilies. Charming service by co-owners Michael Bricker and Pauline Ashworth and their staff complete this picture of bliss. The outside world can seem far away here.

The Phew! factor

Watching the surf pound Knockinaam's deserted beach as the lights of Ireland twinkle in the distance.

Desirable Distractions Walk! Choose your own pace, but walk you must: through delightfully bordered lawns, up and down wooded hills and glens, along blustery cliff tops and by the harbour side. There are many courses for golf lovers too.

Love Bites Knockinaam's secluded but no gastronomic desert: its contemporary Michelin-rated cuisine includes a daily changing four-course 'tasting' menu plus canapés and petit fours. Over 400 wine selections and a vast collection of malt whiskies – for savouring, not for knockin' back! – complete the picture.

Pillow Talk Cosseting is a key word here: exquisitely decorated bedrooms have lots of thoughtful amenities. The two of you might play the numbers game: snuggle down under crisp cotton sheets and watch one of over 100 videos, with a nightcap or three from Michael's collection of over 140 fine single malts or 40 champagnes. Sleep tight.

Getting There From the A75/A77 head to Portpatrick. Two miles past Lochans, turn left at Smokehouse and follow signs.

Minmore House

Glenlivet, Banffshire
AB37 9DB
tel: 01807 590378
fax: 01807 590472
enquiries@minmorehousehotel.com
www.minmorehousehotel.com

Rooms and rates
9 rooms.
Double room for 2 people per night including full breakfast, afternoon tea, dinner and VAT from £180

Managers
Lynne & Victor Janssen

Far from the madding crowd, midway between Elgin, Inverness and Aberdeen, Minmore House is a storybook Scottish hideaway. Delightfully secluded – it stands at the heart of the Glenlivet Crown Estate in miles of glens and forests – it offers stunning views of the Grampian Hills. Surrounded by flower-filled gardens in summer and dusted with snow in winter, the white stone house is filled with homely touches, while the oak-panelled bar stocks over 100 malts. Benji, the Jack Russell, is on hand to greet arriving guests, closely followed by amiable managers Lynne and Victor Janssen.

The Phew! Factor

Just the place for a flirty weekend in the Highlands.

Desirable Distractions The famous Glenlivet Distillery is only two minutes away, while the castles of Fraser, Drum, Crathes and Ballindalloch are close by. You can also try your hand at fly fishing, shooting, cycling, golf or riding.

Love Bites Dinner – making maximum use of fresh local Speyside produce – is served in the intimate candlelit dining room. Feast on tender Aberdeen Angus steak or king scallops baked in a lobster sauce with Noilly Prat. Do leave room for afternoon tea, complete with bobotie sausage rolls and Lynne's famous chocolate whisky cake.

Pillow Talk Ten warm, spacious bedrooms, each individually designed. The Glenlivet Room boasts a huge four-poster and even bigger bay windows. Gaze out at the views (Minmore is a TV-free zone, so you won't be watching telly) or snuggle under feather duvets.

Getting There Minmore House is on the B9008 (reached via the A93 from Aberdeen), just before the Glenlivet Distillery north of Tomintoul.

The Peat Inn

By Cupar
Fife KY15 5LH
tel: 01334 840206
fax: 01334 840530
reception@thepeatinn.co.uk
www.thepeatinn.co.uk

Rooms and rates
8 suites.
Double room for 2 people per night including full breakfast and VAT from £145

Proprietors
David & Patricia Wilson

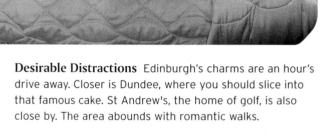

This old coaching post now enjoys a reputation as a first class restaurant. So much so that owners David and Patricia Wilson have extended the original building to provide luxury accommodation for diners wishing to prolong their post-prandial pleasures. Their ethos is dedicated to 'the pleasure of the palate, the eyes, the heart and the soul,' which strikes us as rather nicely encapsulating the notion of the ideal romantic break. Views to 'lighten and renew the heart,' abound in this inviting corner of Fife, where coastal walks, bird life and golfing abound.

The Phew! factor

A little bit of Scotland that's internationally acclaimed for its food, wine and aesthetic comforts.

Desirable Distractions Edinburgh's charms are an hour's drive away. Closer is Dundee, where you should slice into that famous cake. St Andrew's, the home of golf, is also close by. The area abounds with romantic walks.

Love Bites David Wilson is a Chef Laureate of the British Gastronomic Academy and a past winner of the Egon Ronay Wine Cellar of the Year award – so guests are assured of some Bacchanalian high living. The modern cuisine features high quality local specialities, including the freshest sea and river fish.

Pillow Talk Patricia Wilson is a design graduate. She's used her flair to lure guests into a whirl of luxury, with period French furniture, rich fabrics and Italian marble bathrooms with quality aromatics. One guest called this the 'Inn of Great Happiness,' which suggests interesting portents for lovebirds.

Getting There An hour's drive from Edinburgh, the Peat Inn can be reached by taking the M90 to Halbeath and then the A92/A915 towards St Andrews.

Pool House Hotel

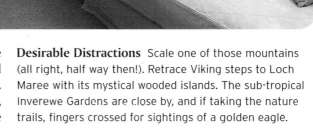

Poolewe, by Achnasheen
Wester Ross IV22 2LD
tel: 01445 781272
fax: 01445 781403
enquiries@poolhousehotel.com
www.poolhousehotel.com

Rooms and rates
4 rooms.
Double room for 2 people
per night including full
breakfast and VAT from
£190 to £330

Proprietors
The Harrison family

Surrounded by rugged mountain backdrops, on the shores of Loch Ewe and alongside its river mouth, Pool House is located in Wester Ross at its most captivating. Around those enticing clear waters are seals, cormorants, herons and otters. In the hotel itself are enticements of other sorts: intimate Victorian splendour lovingly restored by its owners, the Harrison family. While you're languorously ensconced by the drawing room fire with a fine malt in hand (another high point of Highland life) they and the charming staff are at your bidding.

The Phew! factor

From these splendid surrounds look westwards at an amazing Scottish sunset. In winter months the Aurora Borealis brings a twinkle.

Desirable Distractions Scale one of those mountains (all right, half way then!). Retrace Viking steps to Loch Maree with its mystical wooded islands. The sub-tropical Inverewe Gardens are close by, and if taking the nature trails, fingers crossed for sightings of a golden eagle.

Love Bites You will want a table overlooking the loch. Prize-winning fare is on offer: choose from local rope-grown mussels, hill-fed lamb or gamey game. The scallops here are apparently Britain's most amorous. Why? Because they're from the Isle of Ewe (as in 'I Love Ewe'... oh, that gentle Scots humour!).

Pillow Talk The Diadem suite luxuriously duplicates one in the Titanic (the owner is descended from the captain). The only sinking you do, however, is into the 7ft square four-poster, and vast Edwardian bath with glass canopied shower.

Getting There From Inverness (frequent flights from Luton and Gatwick) head towards Ullapool on the A835. Take the A832 for Gairloch to reach the hotel.

The Royal Scotsman

46E Constitution Street
Edinburgh EH6 6RS
tel: 0131 555 1344
fax: 0131 555 1345
bookings@royalscotsman.co.uk
www.royalscotsman.com

Rooms and rates
20 cabins.
Tours (1-4 nights) include all
entertainment, visits and
crew gratuities from £550
per person per night

Managing Director
Stephen Coupe

Conjure up the romantic age of rail travel – when getting there was as much fun as arriving – and you'll picture the splendour of The Royal Scotsman. You'll feel like an honoured guest at a private party on board this sumptuous train, where there is a piper to welcome you aboard at Edinburgh and an Edwardian observation car lined with tartan sofas from which to soak up the unfolding panorama of glens, lochs and coastline outside. Itineraries range from the one-night Wee Dram to the four-night Classic Tour taking in Kyle of Lochalsh and Britain's most scenic stretch of railway.

The Phew! factor

The grandest of Highland flings! You can't beat this for a special celebration.

Desirable Distractions All that jaw-dropping scenery. You'll enjoy visits to places ranging from Inverawe Smokehouse to Ballindalloch – one of Scotland's most romantic castles – the Highland Wildlife Park and Loch Carron, famous for its seals.

Love Bites Epicurean delights are savoured in surroundings to match. Choose to dine à deux or in the convivial company of fellow guests in richly decorated dining cars. You'll enjoy prime Scottish salmon, game and Angus beef at candelabra-lit tables in a restaurant acclaimed as one of Britain's finest.

Pillow Talk Your carriage awaits. The train is stabled each night in a quiet siding or station, and twin-bedded cabins are beautifully decorated in rich mahogany with delicate marquetry. Each has every modern convenience, constant hot water and endless fluffy white towels.

Getting There Tours leave from Edinburgh's Waverley station, where guests have use of the first class lounge.

The Three Chimneys

Colbost, Dunvegan
Isle of Skye IV55 8ZT
tel: 01470 511258
fax: 01470 511358
eatandstay@threechimneys.co.uk
www.threechimneys.co.uk

Rooms and rates
6 suites.
Double room for 2 people
per night including
buffet breakfast and VAT
£175

Proprietors
Eddie & Shirley Spear

Should you travel to this dreamy corner of the Isle of Skye simply for a delicious dinner (and perhaps stay the night); or should you plan ahead to stay a while? We suggest opting for the latter. Friendly owners Eddie and Shirley Spear have injected a sophistication into these white-washed stone and slate cottages that belies expectations. As a result, the chic Three Chimneys has been showered with awards, for both its stylish cuisine and ambience. Recent accolades include a placing (among only five elite addresses in the UK) in *Restaurant Magazine's* 2002 World's 50 Best Restaurants list.

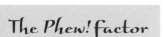

The Phew! factor

Skye at its most heavenly – with shimmering sea views on the doorstep.

Desirable Distractions Skye's rugged north west coastal scenery stretches invitingly from the French windows. Follow your nose along wind-swept beaches complete with basking seals, over hills, lochs and cliffs.

Love Bites The Spears are passionate about food (as you will be after dining here). Their culinary skills and creativity are immediately apparent; critics have lavished praise and prizes. Seafood is a speciality, but prime Scotch beef, lamb and game also figure. Candlelight flickers off the restaurant's rough stone walls. Quite lovely.

Pillow Talk Six split-level suites have king-size beds, CD players and deep double-end baths for two. Fresh modern furnishings are upholstered in linens, suedes and velvets set off by striking contemporary Scots art. Crack open the champers, light a candle and gaze out at a starlit sky from between the sheets.

Getting There When you reach Dunvegan village, take the B884 to Glendale and travel five miles to Colbost.

The Witchery by the Castle

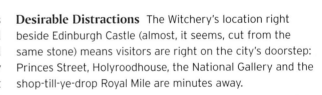

Castlehill, Royal Mile
Edinburgh EH1 2NF
tel: 0131 225 5613
fax: 0131 220 4392
mail@thewitchery.com
www.thewitchery.com

Rooms and rates
6 suites.
Double room for 2 people
per night including continental
breakfast, champagne and
VAT from £195

Proprietor
James Thomson

Opulence takes on a new meaning in this hedonist's heaven in the heart of Edinburgh. Stone floors and tapestries, mysterious shadows and glistening wood panelling create a place once described by a celebrity guest – who we prefer not to indict – as 'the perfect lust den.' The problem comes in deciding which enticement will push your buttons. Will it be The Inner Sanctum or The Old Rectory? The Vestry or The Armoury? Each of these extraordinary suites conspires to create a truly intoxicating setting. No wonder it's a celeb's favourite.

The Phew! factor

What more can we say? Romantic panache from the rafters down.

Desirable Distractions The Witchery's location right beside Edinburgh Castle (almost, it seems, cut from the same stone) means visitors are right on the city's doorstep: Princes Street, Holyroodhouse, the National Gallery and the shop-till-ye-drop Royal Mile are minutes away.

Love Bites Owner James Thomson's Witchery restaurant has become something of an Edinburgh landmark. This is the place for serious prize-winning cuisine. The menu includes Fife crab salad with lime mayonnaise and mango, and pan-roasted fillet of Aberdeen Angus beef with fondant potato. Follow this with the suite course.

Pillow Talk Every lavishly decorated suite has a theatrically indulgent ambience: rampant with plush period textiles and tapestries, with masses of cushions strewn across the beds. Huge roll-top baths are big enough for two. Some bathrooms even have open fires.

Getting There The Witchery is a five-minute taxi ride from Edinburgh's Waverley station.

Wales

St David's

Caernarfon

Llangollen

Aberystwyth

Builth
Wells

Swansea

Cardiff

Why we love Wales

Its mountains and gentle breezes soothe the soul and lift the heart

Green, green hills, sleepy villages, lilting language and ever-present music make this a world apart

If your beloved whispers 'Rwy'n caru ti,' you simply reply 'I love you, too'

"They dined on mince, and slices of quince,
Which they ate with a runcible spoon;
And hand in hand, on the edge of the sand,
They danced by the light of the moon,
The moon!
They danced by the light of the moon."

Edward Lear

The Lake Country House

Llangammarch Wells
Powys LD4 4BS
tel: 01591 620202
fax: 01591 620457
info@lakecountryhouse.co.uk
www.lakecountryhouse.co.uk

Rooms and rates
19 rooms.
Double room for 2 people
per night including full
breakfast and VAT from
£130 to £215

Proprietors
Jean-Pierre & Jan Mifsud

Mid-Wales's characteristically wild scenery has been beautifully tamed here. Tranquillity and charm are twin hallmarks of this elegant and airy Edwardian country house which is furnished with fine antiques and paintings, with fresh flowers everywhere. (Welsh love-spoons are an appropriate decorative touch). Friendly service isn't stinted either. Guests step outside into 50 acres of woods and parkland with manicured lawns, river frontage and a well stocked trout lake where herons and kingfishers swoop. It's quite idyllic; not surprisingly the hotel has won numerous awards.

The Phew! Factor

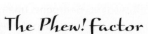

Traditional afternoon tea here is a terrific spread: by the log fire in winter, and under the chestnut trees on warm summer days.

Desirable Distractions Take a romantic riverside walk through the grounds. More active pursuits include tennis, fishing and horse riding. Local attractions include historic castles, a bird reserve and the Black Mountains.

Love Bites The pretty candlelit restaurant sparkles with crystal and silver, and the menu dazzles, too. It's an award-winning fusion of Welsh and English cuisine with a twist. Try specialities such as the local Welsh venison with creamy Savoy cabbage and blackcurrant vinegar sauce. Heavenly.

Pillow Talk In the exquisitely furnished Eugenie suite you'll have your own jacuzzi bath. Soak awhile, then sink back into your richly carved mahogany bed. Peep from the window and you might spot a family of ducks waddling down to the lake.

Getting There The hotel is accessible from the M4. Take the A449 north, then the A40 for Brecon until you join the A470 heading north. Cardiff is 60 miles away.

Llangoed Hall

Llyswen, Brecon
Powys LD3 0YP
tel: 01874 754525
fax: 01874 754545
llangoed_hall_co_wales_uk@compuserve.com
www.llangoedhall.com

Rooms and rates
23 rooms including 3 suites.
Double room for 2 people
per night including full
breakfast and VAT from
£165 to £320

Proprietor
Sir Bernard Ashley

The welcome at Sir Bernard Ashley's imposing Llangoed Hall is wonderfully personal. Charming staff greet guests as if they were entering a private home – albeit a grand one. This is, after all, one of Wales's finest Edwardian country house hotels (whose origins stretch back some 1,400 years). The present, though, marries turn-of-the-century grandeur – big deep sofas, great stone fireplaces, fine antique furniture, library and snooker room as well as Sir Bernard's personal collection of oil paintings. Outside, grounds stretch down to the river.

The Phew! factor

One of the great houses built by architect William Clough-Ellis – recreated by a great designer.

Desirable Distractions Time your stay just right and you could catch the blues at the Brecon jazz festival, or turn a page at Hay-on-Wye's legendary book festival. How about salmon fishing on the Wye, archery on the estate, or stretching your legs on the magnificent Brecon Beacons?

Love Bites The pretty dining room – in shades of lemon and blue – is the perfect setting for meals that celebrate fresh local produce in modern, classic style. An exceptional cellar offers over 300 wines from the old and new worlds. And don't forget tea in the sunny morning room.

Pillow Talk Bedrooms (many with four-posters and high ceilings) are dressed in the best of Sir Bernard Ashley's Elanbach fabrics; there's a real feeling of plush. Each is different and all enjoy thoughtful extras such as fresh fruit, a decanter of sherry and good books.

Getting There Take the M4 from Cardiff or Newport. The hotel is situated on the A470, 11 miles south of Builth Wells and north east of Brecon.

The Old Rectory Country House

Llansanffraid Glan Conwy,
Conwy LL28 5LF
tel: 01492 580611
fax: 01492 584555
info@oldrectorycountryhouse.co.uk
www.oldrectorycountryhouse.co.uk

Rooms and rates
6 rooms.
Double room for 2 people
per night including full
breakfast and VAT from
£119 to £169

Proprietors
Wendy & Michael Vaughan

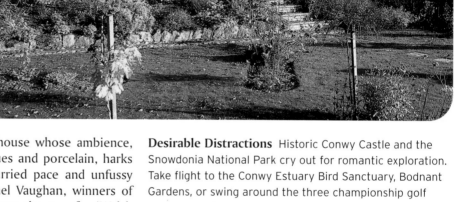

An elegant Georgian country house whose ambience, created by old pictures, antiques and porcelain, harks back to former times of unhurried pace and unfussy calm. Hosts Wendy and Michael Vaughan, winners of many awards, more than deserve the one for 'Welsh Hospitality at its Best', and their outstanding welcome cannot be gainsaid. The comforts they offer are matched by memorable views and terraced gardens that tumble on to lawns stretching out into gorgeous North Wales. Snowdonia and the rugged Welsh coastline await discovery nearby.

The Phew! factor

Panoramic vistas from the front gardens include Conwy Castle, floodlit at night.

Desirable Distractions Historic Conwy Castle and the Snowdonia National Park cry out for romantic exploration. Take flight to the Conwy Estuary Bird Sanctuary, Bodnant Gardens, or swing around the three championship golf courses nearby.

Love Bites Drinks are served in the panelled drawing room, where sometimes a harpist plays. Guests are in for a major treat: Wendy is the first woman in Wales to be awarded a Michelin star. Her notable gastronomy includes monkfish with risotto or Welsh lamb with spinach parcels. At breakfast it's Welsh rarebit – the genuine article.

Pillow Talk Rooms are thoroughly inviting, with nicely appointed bathrooms. The king size four-posters and half-tester beds are lavishly draped and there are lots of extras to hand, including fresh fruit.

Getting There The hotel is on the A470 to Betws-y-Coed, just south of its junction with the A55, and two miles from Llandudno Junction station (London – three hours).

Penally Abbey

Penally, Nr. Tenby
South Pembrokeshire SA70 7PY
tel: 01834 843033
fax: 01834 844714
info@Penally-Abbey.com
www.penally-abbey.com

Rooms and rates
12 rooms.
Double room for 2 people
per night including full
breakfast and VAT from
£120

Proprietors
Steve & Elleen Warren

One of Pembrokeshire's fine listed country houses, Penally Abbey is set high above Carmarthen Bay with views that set the pulse racing. Just a little though: the place itself has a tranquillity that befits a building, part 17th century, with religious antecedents. Once owned by the Jameson whiskey family, Penally Abbey has an unmistakably welcoming air, and ruins of a chapel can be seen in the five acres of picturesque gardens and woodlands. Owners Steve and Elleen Warren have worked hard to imbue the large, airy and elegantly furnished rooms with a sense of laid back comfort.

The Phew! factor

A house whose monastic past doesn't stint on today's worldly pleasures.

Desirable Distractions The Abbey is within a stone's throw of one of Tenby's most beautiful beaches, and the 180 mile Pembrokeshire Coastal Path meanders nearby. Off the coast is Caldey Island, home to a religious community of Cistercian monks. Indoors play snooker, tickle the ivories or swim in the small indoor pool.

Love Bites The pretty candlelit dining room faces the sea, but whichever way the wind's blowing Elleen Warren is cooking up a storm in the kitchen. Her gourmet menu includes regional Pembrokeshire dishes. The cellar doesn't disappoint either.

Pillow Talk Many rooms have four-posters and all have those extra touches such as good sherry and thick towelling robes. Ask for a room in the main house with views over the bay. That said, the adjoining coach house certainly isn't second best.

Getting There From the M4, take the A477 to Tenby. Penally village is just off the A4139 Tenby-Pembroke coast road. The hotel is adjacent to the church, on the village green.

Penmaenuchaf Hall

Penmaenpool, Dolgellau
Gwynedd LL40 1YB
tel: 01341 422129
fax: 01341 422787
relax@penhall.co.uk
www.penhall.co.uk

Rooms and rates
14 rooms.
Double room for 2 people
per night including full
breakfast and VAT from
£116 to £176

Proprietors
Lorraine Fielding & Mark Watson

If Snowdonia National Park is Wales at its loveliest, then Penmaenuchaf could be called a prize within a prize. This handsome Victorian mansion dwells below the Idris mountains and is bounded by 20 acres of terraced gardens overlooking the Mawddach Estuary. The location is idyllic. Above the main entrance a heraldic crest hints that fine things await across the threshold, and guests aren't disappointed. Rooms have the burnished glow of dusky pinks and daffodil yellows with elegant furnishings. There's an air of tranquillity here and the staff are convivial and soothing.

The Phew! factor

Guests have reported 'a naughty half-tester and fabulous fun in that room with the jacuzzi.' Well, now you know.

Desirable Distractions A swing hangs from an old oak tree near the hotel's sunken rose garden. Nearby, discover intriguing gold and slate mines, sandy beaches, pony trekking and a bird hide at Penmaenpool. Or take a ride on the nearby narrow gauge railway (and cling to each other).

Love Bites It's a veritable local lovefest here: tenderest Welsh black beef, the sweetest Bala lamb, wild trout from the Wnion... not forgetting that symbol of national pride, the leek. The chef cooks with regard, and the panelled dining room is a delight.

Pillow Talk The Welsh have always had a good line in poetry; the view across the valley from some of the bedrooms could soon have you waxing lyrical to each other (the place has that sort of effect).

Getting There Approaching Dolgellau on the A470, take the A493 towards Tywyn and Fairbourne. After 3/4 of a mile you will find the entrance drive to Penmaenuchaf Hall.

T'yn Rhos

Llanddeiniolen
Caernarfon LL55 3AE
tel: 01248 670489
fax: 01248 670079
enquiries@tynrhos.co.uk
www.tynrhos.co.uk

Rooms and rates
12 rooms.
Double room for 2 people
per night including full
breakfast and VAT from
£80 to £120

Proprietors
Nigel & Lynda Kettle

The transformation worked by Nigel and Lynda Kettle from humble working farmhouse (with B&B on the side) to the stylish, award-winning T'yn Rhos of today is testimony to their dedication and flair. Over the years this endeavour has seen increasing levels of sophisticated refurbishment, which cleverly hasn't lost the rustic and rural charms of the original. Its location, in a lush plain between Snowdonia and the sea, bounded by fields where sheep and cattle contentedly graze and where ducks and moorhens glide across private lakes, completes this North Wales idyll.

The Phew! Factor

No doubt about it: a lovely Welsh find (now try saying that in Welsh!)

Desirable Distractions Feel the sea breeze in your hair while walking along unspoilt beaches. Explore the historic castles of Caernarfon, Conwy and Beaumaris. Perhaps tackle Mount Snowdon on foot – or by railway track.

Love Bites Notable cooking that highlights the true taste of Wales with numerous specialities using fresh local produce. Enchanting views towards Anglesey from the dining room. Here a meal might include Welsh moules marinières of Menai mussels, which locals say revitalises the libido.

Pillow Talk Take one of the spacious and comfortably furnished doubles in the renovated cottage, set apart from the main building and, say the owners, 'secluded enough to indulge in passionate exchanges without distraction.' Providing you can tear yourself away from those lyrical views.

Getting There Take the A5 west to Bangor, then the A487 towards Caernarfon. Turn off on to the B4547 and follow signs to Llanddeiniolen.

England

Newcastle

Lake District

The North

9

7 6 8
10

5 York

1

Manchester

4 12

Chester

Midshires

13 11

Leicester

24

28 26

East Anglia

Birmingham

Cotswolds

14

Oxford

21

17 18

16 22 23 15

47 19 20

Bath

25 27

London

35 The South 31 38

45 39

46

West Country

37 32 33

36

41

43 29 30

44 34

42 Plymouth 40 Brighton

🥚 The Channel Islands

Guernsey

49 Sark

Jersey

48

Pages 36 - 82

Why we love England

Quaint village pubs, hills and dales, hedgerows and haystacks… so many perfect settings for a kiss!

"What a mischievous devil Love is!"

Samuel Butler

The Devonshire

Bolton Abbey, Skipton
North Yorkshire BD23 6AJ
tel: 01756 710441
fax: 01756 710564
reservations@thedevonshirearms.co.uk
www.devonshirehotels.co.uk

Rooms and rates
41 rooms.
Double room for 2 people
per night including full
breakfast and VAT from
£195 to £345

Managing Director
Jeremy Rata

Owned by one of Britain's great ducal families, this restored former 17th century coaching inn bears the gracious and inimitable touch of the Duke and Duchess of Devonshire. Located within the breathtaking Yorkshire Dales and on the Duke's estate, it exemplifies the innate good taste of an elegant country house. It's strewn with antiques and pictures, counterpointed with award-winning contemporary design features. The hotel's surroundings are equally impressive: the rolling Dales countryside, the magnificent ruins of the 12th century Augustinian priory and miles of footpaths.

The Phew! Factor

Step into the pretty walled cutting garden and pick a posy of fresh flowers. Don't be coy – it's allowed!

Desirable Distractions Will it be the sybaritic indulgences of the luxurious spa; a heavenly traipse around the estate's 12th century priory; a vigorous walk over the fells, or a sightseeing spin in a classic car organised by the hotel? Decisions, decisions!

Love Bites Dine either in the elegant Burlington Restaurant, where head chef Michael Wignall will treat you to star quality ingredients sourced from the estate and matched with fine wines from the impressive 1,200 bin list, or nibble deliciously, but less formally, in the contemporary Bar Brasserie.

Pillow Talk One of the splendid four-posters is so tall you need steps to climb into it. Your heart can skip another beat in the morning with a champagne breakfast in bed, while gazing over Wharfedale's splendid scenery.

Getting There Located on the B6160, north of the junction with the A59, The Devonshire is within easy driving distance of the M1, M62 and M6.

Seaham Hall

Lord Byron's Walk, Seaham
County Durham SR7 7AG
tel: 0191 516 1400
fax: 0191 516 1410
reservations@seaham-hall.com
www.seaham-hall.com

Rooms and rates
19 rooms including 4 suites.
Double room for 2 people
per night including full
breakfast and VAT from
£195 to £500

Proprietors
Tom & Jocelyn Maxfield

If you ever need an excuse for staying close to the heart-stirring moods of the North Sea, you'll find one here: Lord Byron was married at Seaham Hall. What other trysts he may have engaged in during his stay, we can only guess at. Certainly, the views across landscaped cliff-top grounds and gardens would have eased his furrowed brow, or delighted his fanciful heart, whichever mood he was in. Today, owners Tom and Jocelyn Maxfield offer guests a languid luxury manor house whose strikingly designed interior is bound to appeal to the romantic poet in us all.

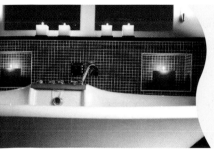

The Phew! factor

A stunning Oriental Spa is being built, whose sensuous and holistic treatments will surely bliss you out.

Desirable Distractions Pamper yourself in the hotel's fabulous new Oriental Spa – billed as the finest in any British hotel. If you can tear yourself away, try a blood-stirring cliff-top walk, a visit to Hadrian's Wall or a browse in Newcastle's cosmopolitan stores.

Love Bites Meals here are a 'must-tell.' Head chef John Connell's three kitchens use fine, fresh ingredients and an eclectic, original style you'll savour. Delicious Thai specialities, taken in the informal setting of the Oriental Spa, are de rigueur.

Pillow Talk 18 individually designed suites, each a veritable gallery of contemporary paintings and drawings. Huge beds. Elaborate electronic indulgences, including 150 downloadable CDs with superb sound. All that, and all-day room service. Do you really want to leave?

Getting There From the A1(M), exit at Junction 62 on the A690. Travel north through Houghton le Spring, then on to the A19 southbound (signposted for Seaham on the B1404).

Waren House Hotel

Waren Mill, Belford
Northumberland NE70 7EE
tel: 01668 214581
fax: 01668 214484
enquiries@warenhousehotel.co.uk
www.warenhousehotel.co.uk

Rooms and rates
11 rooms including 3 suites.
Double room for 2 people
per night including full
breakfast and VAT from
£120 to £195

Proprietors
Peter & Anita Laverack

England's north east coast tends to be overlooked in favour of more obvious destinations. But why? It's glorious. Hordes would descend if they knew about Peter and Anita Laverack's Northumberland gem, beside a bird sanctuary with its sweeping vistas of the Holy Island of Lindisfarne. This charming Georgian house, with its antique-filled interior and six acres of gardens, lawns and woodland, enjoys an enviable peacefulness, bolstered by its mystical location. Guests needn't live monastically however – this is a mecca for disciples of quiet pleasure.

The Phew! Factor

Serene location blessed
with views towards the
Holy Island of Lindisfarne.

Desirable Distractions A good vantage point for exploring Northumberland and the Scottish borders. Lindisfarne, reachable only at low tide, stirs the soul. Great castles like Bamburgh and Alnwick inspire awe, as does Hadrian's Wall. There's also golf, riding and boat trips.

Love Bites Chefs Paul and Graham prepare prize-winning traditional cuisine using excellent local Northumbrian produce. It's prettily served in a candlelit dining room with formally dressed tables, and splendid views from the windows. A well thought out wine list includes 250 bins.

Pillow Talk In the mood for love? Ensuite rooms and suites offer four individual styles to choose from: French, Oriental, Victorian and Edwardian (with views of the Cheviot Hills). Each elegantly furnished room is pleasing, whatever your taste.

Getting There Turn off the A1 at the B1342, heading towards Bamburgh. Turn right at the T-junction in the village of Waren Mill.

The White House Manor

The Village, Prestbury
Cheshire SK10 4HP
tel: 01625 829376
fax: 01625 828627
info@thewhitehouse.uk.com
www.thewhitehouse.uk.com

Rooms and rates
11 rooms.
Double room for 2 people
per night including VAT
from £70 to £120

Proprietors
Ryland & Judith Wakeham

If owners Ryland and Judith Wakeham have one defining characteristic in their hotel, it's undeniably a sense of pizzazz. They've taken a Georgian manor house and transformed the interior into a luxurious private sanctuary. This is perfectly captured in the 11 themed bedrooms which indulge the sensuous, fantastical and possibly a little wicked. Breakfast is served in your room: you may well not wish to leave it during your stay but do try, if only to sample the award-winning fare in the hotel's two separate restaurants just minutes away. The whole experience is delightfully tendered.

The Phew! factor

The Millennium room boasts a futuristic glass bed and its own Turkish steam room. The temperature's definitely rising here.

Desirable Distractions Discover one of Cheshire's great aristocratic country seats such as Tatton, Lyme or Styal. Alternatively, there's plenty of new wealth to be seen in Manchester's posh boutiques and Harvey Nicks.

Love Bites The White House Restaurant celebrates contemporary British cuisine with clean-cut flavours, while the new post-modern Amba is becoming a fashionable hang-out. There's definitely something in the food: we hear that six staff, including two of the chefs, are marrying each other!

Pillow Talk Rooms, all ensuite, are the stuff of fantasy. Try the voluptuous Aphrodite room, the glamorous red and gold Minerva, the dramatic Glyndebourne with its sophisticated music centre or the Crystal Room, gleaming beneath its chandelier.

Getting There From the M6 take Exit 17 to the A534 towards Congleton, then the A536 to Prestbury. White House Manor is located just over the bridge.

The Yorke Arms

Ramsgill-in-Nidderdale, Harrogate
North Yorkshire HG3 5RL
tel: 01423 755243
fax: 01423 755330
enquiries@yorke-arms.co.uk
www.yorke-arms.co.uk

Rooms and rates
14 rooms.
Double room for 2 people
per night including full
breakfast, dinner and VAT
from £170 to £300

Proprietors
Bill & Frances Atkins

Make the romantic journey north from Pateley Bridge, past the glittering man-made waters of Gouthwaite Reservoir in the beautiful Nidderdale Valley, and you'll find a gem of the Yorkshire Dales: The Yorke Arms. Once an 18th century coaching house and shooting lodge, now in the creative hands of Bill and Frances Atkins, this creeper-clad, rough-stone haven exudes a simple country grace and the sort of welcome Yorkshire folk are famous for. One of Britain's acclaimed restaurants with rooms, it has made a name for fabulous cuisine and fine wines.

The Phew! factor

Delicious and imaginative dishes will have you sharing spoonfuls across the table...

Desirable Distractions Tarrying in a landscape of such beauty, does one really need distractions? A couple – just to gild the lily – include the mystical Brimham rocks and Fountains Abbey. Historic York, fine country houses and the genteel delights of Harrogate's tea rooms also beckon.

Love Bites Prize-winning dishes with big, bold, clear flavours without frills or folderol, thanks to the culinary skill and presentation master chef Frances brings to her work. Breakfasts are well done too, while the wine list (among the AA's top 30) showcases over 300 bins.

Pillow Talk You won't have far to stagger after a post-prandial snifter in the sofa-stuffed sitting room. Simplicity is the keynote in the 14 ensuite rooms (one boasting a four-poster), each of which has its own character and comforts.

Getting There From Skipton on the A59, take the B6265 to Pateley Bridge and head left towards Ramsgill, where the hotel is situated by the green.

Gilpin Lodge

Crook Road, Windermere,
Cumbria LA23 3NE
tel: 015394 88818
fax: 015394 88058
hotel@gilpin-lodge.co.uk
www.gilpin-lodge.co.uk

Rooms and rates
14 rooms.
Double room for 2 people
per night including full
breakfast and VAT from
£110.

Proprietors
John & Christine Cunliffe

Love was in the air long before the award-winning Gilpin Lodge became John and Christine Cunliffe's idea of a perfect Lakeland hotel. Sweethearts as students, they bought the property – which had once been John's grandmother's home – and set about the task of refurbishing it with studied zeal. Their enthusiasm fills every room with a warmth and style that makes visitors feel quickly at home. Indeed, the rooms are so comfortable and so suffused with romantic tranquillity that guests have often spontaneously extended their stay. So might you.

The Phew! factor

You don't win a 'Lakeland Hotel of the Year' award for nothing!

Desirable Distractions Float through Lakeland's mesmerising countryside – by car, by boat, on foot over the fells or even by hot-air balloon. Or visit famous homes – Holker Hall, Sizergh Castle or Levens Hall – nearby.

Love Bites 'Food is our obsession,' say the Cunliffes. And thank goodness: diners are offered masterful creations such as roasted Périgord quail, with boudin of foie gras mousse, sautéed wild mushrooms and ruby port jus. Make room for the Charlotte Muscovite with white chocolate sorbet and candied raspberries.

Pillow Talk Individually furnished rooms boast antiques, bold, colourful fabrics and a vast array of creature comforts: soaps, gels, body lotions and that quintessential British pick-me-up, tea. The stronger stuff is in the mini-bar (and it's reasonably priced, too).

Getting There Leave the M6 at Junction 36 and take the A590/A591. At the roundabout north of Kendal, take the first exit (B5284) and Gilpin Lodge is five miles on the right.

Holbeck Ghyll

Holbeck Lane, Windermere
Cumbria LA23 1LU
tel: 015394 32375
fax: 015394 34743
stay@holbeckghyll.com
www.holbeckghyll.com

Rooms and rates
20 rooms.
Double room for 2 people
per night including breakfast,
Michelin star dinner and VAT
from £170 to £300

Proprietors
David & Patricia Nicholson

Sitting right at the heart of the region that inspired the poet Wordsworth, Holbeck Ghyll's enviable position overlooking Lake Windermere and the Langdale Fells quite takes your breath away. This 19th century hunting lodge (once the home of Lord Lonsdale, the 'Boxing' Earl), is such a fine example of Cumbrian comforts that it's won many prestigious awards. The oak panelled entrance with its log fire sets the tone, while the recently expanded spa and bedrooms with breathtaking lake views make the place a knock-out.

The Phew! Factor

The warmest of welcomes – and those lakeland views – definitely put the Wow into Windermere.

Desirable Distractions Wander lonely as a cloud through the hotel's dreamy woodlands; take a lakeland cruise for another perspective; then rejuvenate some more with a treatment in the spa. Visit Wordsworth's home and also that of writer Beatrix Potter.

Love Bites Bag a window table for amazing vistas – in fine weather French doors open on to a patio, perfect for dining. The fusion of English and French cuisine is outstandingly good: dishes such as roast quail with onion compote and truffle jus have helped win a Michelin star. The chef will also serve a private dinner in your room.

Pillow Talk 'Peter Rabbit in The Lodge' is also called the Honeymoon and Anniversary room. No wonder. A generous four-poster swathed in lush chintz... a spa bath built for two... a wide French window opening on to a balcony where you can sit and gaze at lakeside and woods.

Getting There Holbeck Ghyll is located just off the A591 to Windermere, minutes from Junction 36 of the M6.

Lovelady Shield

Alston, Cumbria
CA9 3LF
tel: 01434 381203
fax: 01434 381515
enquiries@lovelady.co.uk
www.lovelady.co.uk

Rooms and rates
10 rooms.
Double room for 2 people
per night including full
breakfast and VAT from
£140 to £180

Proprietors
Peter & Marie Haynes

The name Lovelady Shield has a pretty romantic ring to it – and reality doesn't disappoint. Nudging England's highest market town, this pretty Georgian house is approached via a secluded drive along three acres of garden. Amid the rolling fells of the High Pennines, on the banks of the River Nent the hotel is shielded by woods and hills. For friendly owners Peter and Marie Haynes, their hotel is palpably a labour of love; guests are encouraged to settle into this elegant little haven and feel 'miles away from the mad rushing world.' Romantic enough? We'll say.

The Phew! factor

A stunning position. All bedrooms look across the valley towards majestic Cumbrian fells.

Desirable Distractions The usual country pursuits plus some great walking: the Pennine Way and Hadrian's Wall are easily reached. If you run out of puff, the half hour tootle over to Lake Ullswater has won the AA's vote as one of the world's top ten drives.

Love Bites The Haynes aim to serve food to fondly remember them by, and master chef Barrie Gordon's menu utilising top local produce is a winner. What's more, the impressive wine list includes 104 bins. Make room for a hearty Cumberland breakfast too.

Pillow Talk You may only have eyes for each other, but that shouldn't stop you from wanting to gaze at those views – all bedrooms have them. Rooms are comfortable and warmly furnished, and some have four-posters. Just the place to cosy up.

Getting There The hotel lies a few miles east of Alston. The entrance to the drive is at the junction of the A689 and the B6294.

The Pheasant

Bassenthwaite Lake, Nr.
Cockermouth, Cumbria CA13 9YE
tel: 017687 76234
fax: 017687 76002
info@the-pheasant.co.uk
www.the-pheasant.co.uk

Rooms and rates
13 rooms including 3 suites.
Double room for 2 people
per night including full
breakfast and VAT from
£100 to £140

Proprietor
Matthew Wylie

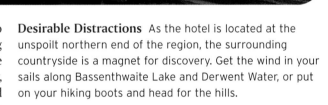

The Lake District isn't short of devotees who return to recharge batteries year after year. There's strong competition, but many not surprisingly fly back to The Pheasant. This mellow inn enjoys 500 years of history, and its charm seems to ooze out of those polished walls. That patina is carried throughout: soft, cosy, welcoming. Lounges look on to charming gardens at the rear of the building. Pretty villages, antique shops and the region's famous fells await exploration outside the door. Having visited, we're sure you'll come back again and again.

The Phew! factor

The mellow bar – all oak settles, wooden beams, polished knick-knacks and log fires – is a true Lakeland hostelry.

Desirable Distractions As the hotel is located at the unspoilt northern end of the region, the surrounding countryside is a magnet for discovery. Get the wind in your sails along Bassenthwaite Lake and Derwent Water, or put on your hiking boots and head for the hills.

Love Bites It's a pretty beamed dining room (there's also a private one) where chef Malcolm Ennis cooks many local Cumbrian specialities. Traditional fare flirts agreeably with nouvelle cuisine: it looks stunning on the plate and tastes it too. Regulars come from miles around.

Pillow Talk All 13 bedrooms have recently been refurbished to high standards, and bathrooms with power showers deliver a good blast of hot or cold. The mood is pretty, fresh and flower-filled and you can awake to a good early morning brew served in your room.

Getting There Leave the M6 at Junction 40 and take the A66 for Keswick and North Lakes. After Keswick, head towards Cockermouth. Follow signposts on the A66.

The Samling

Ambleside Road, Windermere
Cumbria LA23 1LR
tel: 015394 31922
fax: 015394 30400
info@thesamling.com
www.thesamling.com

Rooms and rates
10 rooms including 2 suites.
Double room for 2 people
per night including full
breakfast and VAT from
£135 to £295

Proprietors
Tom & Jocelyn Maxfield

The Samling – where poet William Wordsworth used to pay his rent on his nearby home, Dove Cottage – is an inspirational destination for romantics, standing as it does in landscaped grounds high above Windermere, one of Britain's loveliest lakes. The hotel comprises an intimate main building surrounded by guest cottages, pulled together by a style that combines classic good taste with a fresh perspective and modern twist. There's none of that snooty nostalgic stuff here, say the owners, and its magical and historical associations are left intact.

The Phew! factor

What views! Wake each day to see the lake as placid as a sleeping cat, or playful as a lamb.

Desirable Distractions Imagine a morning on horseback; a snooze in a boat; a picnic on a fell; a canoe to an island; paragliding after tea; watching the sunset from an outdoor hot tub. It really is that lyrical.

Love Bites There's a lightness of touch in the cooking, with ingredients whose freshness seems to leap from the plate. The hotel's cellars contain some fine selections that hold their own under some pretty expert noses. Breakfast is a treat too.

Pillow Talk Many of the duplex suites are located in individual cottages and have spectacular views over the lake. Because it's so private, guests have the feeling they're cocooned in their own little world: elegantly decorated, with open fires, and just the place for breakfast in bed.

Getting There Leave the M6 at Junction 36. At the large roundabout take the second exit (A591). After two miles you will pass Lake Windermere. The hotel is 300 yards further on.

Hambleton Hall

Hambleton, Oakham, Rutland
Leicestershire LE15 8TH
tel: 01572 756991
fax: 01572 724721
hotel@hambletonhall.com
www.hambletonhall.com

Rooms and rates
17 rooms.
Double room for 2 people
per night including
continental breakfast and
VAT from £180 to £600

General manager
Keith Raxter

Owners Tim and Steffa Hart promised they would work magic when converting this Victorian mansion with its commanding position over Rutland Water. The spell has worked, and the hotel is now recognised as one of the best outside London. Staff make guests feel cosseted, while the classically decorated country house interior and easy comforts add to that sense of being somewhere special. The lakeside setting is tailor-made for unwinding. The owners quite obviously don't rest on their laurels, and it shows: people return here time and again.

The Phew! Factor

Retreat to the purpose-built croquet pavilion with its own bedroom suite. What you play is up to you.

Desirable Distractions Either stay put, revelling in Hambleton's dreamy location, or stroll around the lake. Strike out to Burghley and Belton, historic country houses. Hunt down antiques or make a diverting day trip to Cambridge and Ely.

Love Bites It's a pretty dining room, and head chef Aaron Patterson prepares a menu that's strongly seasonal. As a respecter of tip-top ingredients, he ensures the accent is fully on flavour, starting with truffles in January, wild salmon in summer, chanterelles in autumn. Sommelier Dominique Baduel makes choosing wines fun.

Pillow Talk Heart shaped shortbread and fresh flowers greet guests in each of the individually decorated rooms. Sink into one of the canopied or four-poster beds and stretch to take in those fabulous lake views.

Getting There Hambleton Hall is reached via the A1 (exit at the A606 for Oakham.) Rail travellers should use Peterborough or Kettering, and the branch line to Oakham.

Riber Hall

Matlock
Derbyshire DE4 5JU
tel: 01629 582795
fax: 01629 580475
info@riber-hall.co.uk
www.riber-hall.co.uk

Rooms and rates
14 rooms.
Double room for 2 people
per night including
continental breakfast and
VAT from £127 to £170

Proprietor
Alex Biggin

Some 30 years ago Alex Biggin saw the potential of this historic but derelict 15th century Derbyshire manor house in the foothills of the Pennines, and breathed life into it. The grounds, which include an orchard, buttercup meadows and gardens with rare and exotic plants have been lovingly cultivated. The building's stonework and mullioned exterior have undergone considerate restoration; the interior has been recreated with charming period furnishings and oozes quiet comfort. There is many a peaceful corner to cosy up in.

The Phew! factor

The mad, bad world seems miles away as you stroll through the flower-scented walled garden. Listen out for bird-song.

Desirable Distractions Explore the area's famous caverns and lakes – Heights of Abraham, Castleton and Carsington Water. Or potter round the local potteries. Then there are those great Halls to plunder visually – Haddon, Hardwick and Chatsworth.

Love Bites A pretty room in pale blues and golds with antique furniture and heraldic embellishments looks over fields and valleys. The kitchen delivers award-winning dishes, such as saddle of venison with glazed chestnuts and juniper berries, accompanied by tip-top wines.

Pillow Talk Welcoming suites, some with whirlpools and four-posters into which staff will happily slip hot water bottles. (Hopefully passion will render this unnecessary). Try not to repeat the feat of one amorous couple, who put their feet through the carved panelled headboard!

Getting There From the M1, take Junction 28 to Matlock, continuing along the A615 to Tansley. From there, Alders Lane winds towards Riber Hall.

Stapleford Park

Stapleford
Leicestershire LE14 2EF
tel: 01572 787522
fax: 01572 787651
reservations@stapleford.co.uk
www.stapleford.co.uk

Rooms and rates
51 rooms including 2 suites.
Double room for 2 people
per night including full
breakfast, newspaper and
VAT from £210 to £581

General Manager
William Boulton-Smith

This stately home, surrounded by 500 acres of parkland designed by Capability Brown, was until recently owned by just two aristocratic families for almost 600 years. It's the perfect place to feel like a spoiled house guest at a splendid sporting country estate. The impressively appointed interior filled with fine antiques and family portraits exudes a rich, lordly atmosphere, without forsaking friendliness and informality. Each of the 51 bedrooms is a lavish pièce de résistance showcasing the talents of a top interior designer. What's more, staff know exactly how to pamper you!

The Phew! factor

Sporting estate whose palatial interiors are enhanced by a gym and luxurious health and beauty spa.

Desirable Distractions Where to start? Within the grounds there's a school of falconry; fly fishing on the trout lake; an 18-hole golf course; archery and shooting; tennis and riding; off-road driving; boules and croquet. A new holistic health spa opens in 2003.

Love Bites The main dining room is resplendent with 17th century decoration by Grinling Gibbons. Executive chef Martin Carter uses organic ingredients with real passion: British style cuisine is lightened by Asian and Caribbean influences 'where maximum flavours, whether subtle or strong, are enticed out.'

Pillow Talk Top designers from David Hicks and Nina Campbell to companies like Pirelli, Mulberry and Crabtree and Evelyn have stamped their distinctive style on each room – from classic to dreamy to downright funky.

Getting There Approach via the A1(M), taking the A606 for Oakham and Melton Mowbray. A right hand turn midway between the two towns leads to Stapleford.

Studley Priory

Horton-cum-Studley
Oxford OX33 1AZ
tel: 01865 351203
fax: 01865 351613
res@studley-priory.co.uk
www.studley-priory.co.uk

Rooms and rates
18 rooms including 1 suite.
Double room for 2 people
per night including full
breakfast and VAT from
£165 to £300

Proprietor
Jeremy Parke

This magnificent Elizabethan manor house, set in masses of verdant woodland overlooking the Chilterns and the Vale of Aylesbury, was originally a Benedictine nunnery. Drenched in romantic history, with the heraldic arms of resident families since 1561 adorning the hall walls, Studley Priory's ancient arched and beamed ceilings – set off with modern luxurious soft furnishings – are wholly welcoming. It's a superb location, too, just seven miles from Oxford and its dreaming spires. Elizabethan-minded lovers will want to tarry here awhile.

The Phew! factor

Room 26 has a magnificent four-poster bed with views over the gardens, and a double jacuzzi bath to stir the blood.

Desirable Distractions Stay-at-home diversions include a croquet lawn and tennis court. Further afield you'll find Woodstock and Blenheim Palace with their Churchillian associations and – if you can't resist a designer bargain – Bicester Shopping Village.

Love Bites Take pre-dinner drinks in the cosy oak-panelled Victorian bar before enjoying beautifully presented modern English fare (and an outstanding wine list) in the candlelit Croke restaurant. Down a post-prandial brandy in front of crackling fires in winter.

Pillow Talk Studley Priory's history dates back to the 16th century, and every individually styled and spacious room is beautifully appointed with rich soft furnishings and superb antiques. Many have jacuzzi baths, and all have the 21st century comforts you'd expect.

Getting There Leave the M40 at Junction 8, and follow signs for Horton-cum-Studley village. The hotel is at the top of the hill on the right.

Burford House

99 High Street, Burford
Oxfordshire OX18 4QA
tel: 01993 823151
fax: 01993 823240
stay@burfordhouse.co.uk
www.burfordhouse.co.uk

Rooms and rates
8 rooms including 1 suite.
Double room for 2 people
per night including full
breakfast and VAT from
£95 to £130

Proprietors
Simon & Jane Henty

You'll find this little prize-winning townhouse hotel at the heart of one of the Cotswolds' most picturesque towns. It's Bed and Breakfast at its best – having deservedly won the English Tourism Council Gold Award. This Tudor gem – all low ceilings, oak beams and leaded windows – possesses a nicely fuzzy echo of times past. Time present, however is stylishly delivered by owners Simon and Jane Henty. They have imbued the antique-filled premises with an appealing cosiness and intimacy that strikes exactly the right note. Just the place for a few days in the Cotswolds.

The Phew! factor

Lolling in a deep free-standing Victorian roll-top bath built for two. Better still, with some bubbly within reach.

Desirable Distractions A quintessential British beauty spot, this. So borrow the hotel's bikes and pedal through Burford's history; then take in Blenheim Palace, Oxford and Shakespeare's birthplace nearby. Contemplate the Bard's words on love.

Love Bites Dinner isn't served, but the hotel's gourmet breakfasts and traditional afternoon teas cannot be bettered. Only the best local produce is served, either in the pretty blue dining room or in the charming courtyard. Burford itself is crammed with delightful dining spots.

Pillow Talk Bedrooms are individually furnished with thoughtful extras. The four-posters and king-size doubles might well garner more attention than the books and magazines supplied beside them. Attention to detail is the keynote here.

Getting There Burford is easily reached via the M40 from London. Turn right at the roundabout and you're in the High Street.

The Castle Inn

Castle Combe Nr. Chippenham
Wiltshire SN14 7HN
tel: 01249 783030
fax: 01249 782315
res@castle-inn.co.uk
www.hatton-hotels.co.uk

Rooms and rates
11 rooms.
Double room for 2 people
per night including full
breakfast and VAT from
£95 to £165

Proprietor
Mark Bullows

If you stumbled upon Wiltshire's Castle Combe out of nowhere, you might feel you'd landed on a Hollywood film set, so vividly does it project the rose-tinted view of a perfect English village. But it's real enough – right down to every limestone brick of the 15th century timber-beamed mossy roofed cottages, medieval church, cobbled streets and babbling stream. This delightful hostelry has an ambience that continues the conspiracy of a time-warp, repelling some of the worst of 21st century craziness and replacing it with the best of antiquated indulgence.

The Phew! Factor

Chocolate-box cuteness
that's perfect for
sweethearts!

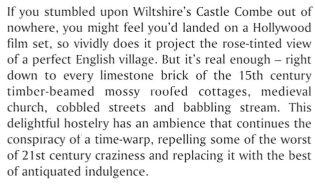

Desirable Distractions Start by crossing the 'Roman' bridge for splendid walks along the Bybrook valley as a prelude to exploring this area of Outstanding Natural Beauty. Also nearby are pretty Cotswold villages, historic country houses and Bath's venerable sights.

Love Bites Tuck into both contemporary and classic dishes: there's a five-course gourmet menu accompanied by select wines (though since this is an inn, it's a place to sup good ales!). There's also a nice conservatory and patio.

Pillow Talk Charming ensuites whose original interior of heavy oak beams and low ceilings is comfortably propped up by modern creature comforts. Guests get all that 'olde worlde' character alongside today's sybaritic pleasures like whirlpool baths and fluffy robes. Luxury toiletries and fresh fruit are laid on too.

Getting There From London, leave the M4 at Junction 17, heading for Chippenham. Join the A420 then turn on to the B4039 for Castle Combe.

Hatton Court

Upton Hill, Upton St Leonards
Nr. Cheltenham GL4 8DE
tel: 01452 617412
fax: 01452 612945
res@hatton-court.co.uk
www.hatton-hotels.co.uk

Rooms and rates
45 rooms including 3 suites.
Double room for 2 people
per night including full
breakfast and VAT from
£115 to £190

General manager
Rob Aldridge

Built of honey-coloured local stone in 17th century style, creeper-clad Hatton Court retains all the character beloved by those seeking the ambience of a bygone age. Set in the heart of one of England's most richly romantic regions, not far from Cheltenham Spa and the cathedral city of Gloucester, this enticing Cotswold hotel has been lovingly pepped up with all today's necessary accoutrements and mod cons. It's a gorgeously comfortable place; one where romance will blossom as sure as the country flowers in the surrounding grounds.

The Phew! Factor

'A hotel should rely on standards rather than standardisation,' say the owners. Hear, hear!

Desirable Distractions Not to be missed are the Rococo Gardens in Painswick, 'The Queen of the Cotswolds.' Sudeley and Berkeley castles are worth exploring, as is Westonbirt Arboretum.

Love Bites Hatton Court's Carrington's restaurant is recognised as one of the area's finest. Its elegant warm interior is complemented by efficient and friendly service. Choose your wine from the extensive selection in the wine shop, one of this interesting establishment's more unusual features.

Pillow Talk Many of the individually decorated rooms have whirlpool baths, and scrumptious extras await such as fresh fruit, mineral water, confectionery (watch that waistline!) and a hot beverage tray. If you do need to burn off calories, try the health suite's sauna or mini gym.

Getting There Leave the M5 at Junction 11a (or J18 of the M4). Take the A46 to Painswick and the B4073 towards Gloucester. Hatton Court is three miles on the left.

The King's Arms

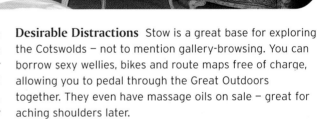

Market Square, Stow-on-the-Wold
Gloucestershire GL54 1AF
tel: 01451 830364
fax: 01451 830602
info@kingsarms-stowonthewold.co.uk
www.kingsarms-stowonthewold.co.uk

Rooms and rates
10 rooms.
Double room for 2 people
per night including full
breakfast and VAT from
£90 to £120

General Manager
Louise Robinson

Located in historic Stow-on-the-Wold in the heart of the Cotswolds, The King's Arms combines refined taste with amiable surroundings, and is the perfect nest for lovebirds looking for a home from home. You can't fail to be smitten by this mellow, Cotswold stone building, with its welcoming rooms and food drummed up by one of the UK's leading chefs. The pub even played host to the legendary (and headless) king and cad, Charles I on 8th May, 1645. Rumour has it that certain loved ones accompanied him, but we wouldn't encourage that sort of behaviour.

The Phew! factor

Great location, great rooms and great food – with a friendliness as warm as the log fire.

Desirable Distractions Stow is a great base for exploring the Cotswolds – not to mention gallery-browsing. You can borrow sexy wellies, bikes and route maps free of charge, allowing you to pedal through the Great Outdoors together. They even have massage oils on sale – great for aching shoulders later.

Love Bites The King's Arms likes to pamper its guests – so why not enjoy dinner behind the bedroom's closed door? The chef will deliver delicious dishes direct to your room: just the place to savour and devour.

Pillow Talk Treat yourself to a night in and watch a romantic movie on your state-of-the-art flat screen TV. Each room has its own television and stereo and, for those times when there's nothing on (the screen, that is) they'll even provide video players.

Getting There Stow-on-the-Wold is on the A429, and is easily reached from Cheltenham, Stratford-upon-Avon, Bath and Oxford.

Lower Slaughter Manor

Lower Slaughter
Gloucestershire GL54 2HP
tel: 01451 820456
fax: 01451 822150
lowsmanor@aol.com
www.lowerslaughter.co.uk

Rooms and rates
13 rooms including 3 suites.
Double room for 2 people
per night including full
breakfast and VAT from
£220 to £395

Proprietors
Roy & Daphne Vaughan

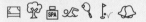

This imposing 17th century stone-built house overlooking manicured lawns, splendid trees and a walled garden containing an ancient dovecote epitomises the charm and perfectly preserved antiquity of the Cotswolds. Past meets present at Lower Slaughter Manor in a way that owners Roy and Daphne Vaughan have pulled off in great style. The immaculate interior epitomises country house chic with plaster ceilings and marble chimney pieces, fine antiques and pictures. Friendliness and relaxed formality combine here to create a real sense of occasion.

The Phew! Factor

Don't be fooled – the name may be 'Lower' but the rich country house atmosphere here reaches the heights.

Desirable Distractions You'll find a croquet lawn, putting green, all-weather tennis court and indoor pool in the grounds. Not far away are picturesque Cotswold villages, Cheltenham racecourse, Stratford-upon-Avon and the grandeur of Blenheim Palace, Warwick and Sudeley castles.

Love Bites The elegantly appointed main dining room is a temple to serious award-winning cuisine using excellent local and continental produce. Fish is beautifully done here. Guests are spoiled by a huge wine list too, with some 800 selections from old and new worlds.

Pillow Talk Bedrooms – some with four-posters – have their own distinct personality but are unified by plush chintzes, damask and soft furnishings. Decanters of sherry, home-made biscuits, fruit and toffees beckon. Smoked salmon and champagne are just a call away.

Getting There Take Junction 15 (M40) or Junction 15 (M4) and follow the A419 to the A429. The Manor is on the right as you enter Lower Slaughter from the A429.

The Plough at Clanfield

Bourton Road, Clanfield
Oxfordshire OX18 2RB
tel: 01367 810222
fax: 01367 810596
ploughatclanfield@hotmail.com
www.room4romance.com

Rooms and rates
12 rooms including 1 suite.
Double room for 2 people
per night including full
breakfast and VAT from
£115 to £135

Proprietors
John & Rosemary Hodges

Built of honey-coloured stone and dating back to 1560, The Plough at Clanfield is a real gem – looking almost untouched by time. But in the hands of John and Rosemary Hodges, this timelessness has been lovingly transformed into one of the Cotswolds' most welcoming hotels, with a beguiling mix of old and new. The spacious lounge, with its voluminous sofas and oversized armchairs set around a magnificent Tudor fireplace, is just the spot to draw you in for a cosy cuddle on cold days. Outside, there's a lovely garden for warm summer afternoons.

The Phew! factor

A rural retreat for the
romantic at heart.

Desirable Distractions Location is everything in the Cotswolds, and The Plough is perfectly placed at its heart. Exhilarating country walks and pretty villages are everywhere. Oxford, Shakespeare's Stratford-upon-Avon and Bath are within easy striking distance.

Love Bites The Plough's Shires Restaurant has a lot going for it: the best of local produce in an à la carte menu designed to seduce even the fussiest of tastes. Attentive staff and an extensive cellar of fine wines make candlelit dinners even more delightful.

Pillow Talk Choose between old-world rooms in the original house or spacious quarters in the new wing – all individually decorated in keeping with the special character of the house. Four-poster beds cry out to be slept in, while a decanter of sherry awaits your pleasure.

Getting There The hotel is at the edge of Clanfield village, at the junction of the A4095 and B4020, between Witney and Faringdon, 15 miles west of Oxford.

The Red Lion

Lower High St, Chipping Campden
Gloucestershire GL55 6AS
tel: 01386 840760
fax: 01386 849134
info@redlion-chippingcampden.co.uk
www.redlion-chippingcampden.co.uk

Rooms and rates
5 rooms.
Double room for 2 people
per night including full
breakfast and VAT from
£62.50 to £82.50

General Manager
John Taylor

Sitting proud in the centre of Chipping Campden, close to the site of the town's ancient sheep market, The Red Lion offers an oasis of calm for couples keen to escape urban stresses. It's a honeycomb of winding corridors, quirky ceilings (watch your head!) and nooks and crannies, complete with traditional Cotswold stone walls and flagstone floors oozing history. The bar offers a genuinely warm welcome – and you can snuggle in your own quiet corner before retiring to your room upstairs. Be sure first to sample the restaurant, whose creations are guaranteed to inspire the holiday mood…

The Phew! Factor

The premier bedroom
features a four-poster and
enormous corner bath.
Water lovely way to go!

Desirable Distractions Time to clasp your partner's hand and meander through picture-postcard Chipping Campden. Enjoy getting lost in the winding streets and narrow lanes of the Cotswolds. You'll need your energy, so tank up on a traditional cream tea.

Love Bites This is a traditional eating house with a passion for good food. Menus dazzle with dishes from Norman and Anglo Saxon times, as well as Mrs Beeton-style favourites like hotpots and pies. Fruit and vegetables are hand-picked each morning. Savour the chef's talents: he enjoys chatting to house guests, so get acquainted.

Pillow Talk Big is beautiful here – so snuggle down beneath the 16th century beams in generous fluffy duvets and beds. Dream, perhaps, of a medieval courtship, when men wore tights and women had chastity belts…

Getting There Chipping Campden is reached via the B4632 from Cheltenham and Stratford-upon-Avon, or the A44 from Evesham and the M5.

The Snooty Fox

Market Place, Tetbury
Gloucestershire GL8 8DD
tel: 01666 502436
fax: 01666 503479
res@snooty-fox.co.uk
www.hatton-hotels.co.uk

Rooms and rates
12 rooms.
Double room for 2 people
per night including full
breakfast and VAT from
£95 to £170

General manager
Sara Clark

In the heart of the Cotswolds' postcard prettiness lies Tetbury, both a historic market town and designated conservation area. The Prince of Wales chose this locale for his country estate, so you know there's lots going for it. It also has The Snooty Fox, a coaching inn dating from the 16th century with a wealth of original brick, stone and timber features. This place has charm in buckets, and makes an ideal base for exploring the area's many sleepy villages, gardens and stately homes. And that familiar looking couple over there in the corner… it's not, you know… *them?*

The Phew! factor

Cotswold coaching inn
riding high on charm.

Desirable Distractions An ideal place to forage for antiques in pretty villages, and seek out stately homes such as Owlpen and Chavenage. Prince Charles's Highgrove estate is almost next door, and you'll find magnificent trees at Westonbirt Arboretum.

Love Bites The atmosphere in the stone-walled bar and restaurant is informal, but the cooking's certainly not casual. Find a cosy corner to sip local ale by the inglenook or enjoy freshly prepared and imaginative home-cooked specials.

Pillow Talk 12 nicely appointed and characterful rooms, many with gently sloping floors and oak beams: two have four-posters. Several have whirlpool baths, while all have those little indulgences we crave but don't always find, like fluffy bathrobes and luxury toiletries.

Getting There Follow signs to Tetbury from Junctions 17/18 of the M4 or Junction 13 of the M5. The Snooty Fox sits in the marketplace in the town centre.

The Swan at Bibury

Bibury, Nr. Cirencester
Gloucestershire GL7 5NW
tel: 01285 740695
fax: 01285 740473
swanhot1@swanhotel-cotswolds.co.uk
www.swanhotel.co.uk

Rooms and rates
20 rooms.
Double room for 2 people
per night including full
breakfast and VAT from
£124.50 to £260

General manager
John Stevens

The Victorian aesthete William Morris called Bibury the prettiest village in England. Many would still agree over a century later, despite vigorous competition. It lies at the heart of the Cotswolds and The Swan itself is enviably positioned. A cluster of ivy-clad buildings in characteristic yellow stonework with a flower-filled courtyard, it overlooks the River Coln's weeping willows. Rooms are cosily furnished in traditional style – the aim is 'to cosset' – and according to one well-travelled couple's recent comment, 'standards of friendliness and service exceed anywhere else we have stayed.'

The Phew! factor

Is this place to die for?
Is it ever!

Desirable Distractions This corner of the country is chocolate-box cute with scrumptious looking villages that cry out for exploration. Otherwise there's Bath, Stratford-upon-Avon and Westonbirt Arboretum. Guests can also bliss out in the luxurious Le Spa Health and Fitness Club.

Love Bites Dinner is beautifully served in the formal surrounds of the Signet Room, where chef Shaun Naen cooks award-winning modern British cuisine with classical influences. Ingredients are locally sourced; trout, for example, is caught from the famous Bibury Trout Farm. Meals are also taken in the intimate brasserie.

Pillow Talk Bedrooms are all individually furnished (some with four-posters) with a nice plush feel. Bathrooms are equally lavish; some are eye-catchingly tiled with twin basins and a jacuzzi. Nothing for it but to slide into those whirling waters and later slip into a plush towelling robe.

Getting There The hotel is situated on the B4425, seven miles north of Cirencester and nine miles south of Burford.

The Hoste Arms

The Green, Burnham Market
Norfolk PE31 8HD
tel: 01328 738777
fax: 01328 730103
reception@hostearms.co.uk
www.hostearms.co.uk

Rooms and rates
35 rooms including 15 suites.
Double room for 2 people
per night including full
breakfast and VAT from
£90 to £150

Proprietors
Paul & Jeanne Whittome

Nelson once visited this North Norfolk inn, and no matter whether he was accompanied by his lover Emma Hamilton, it's certainly worth a dalliance today. Owners Paul and Jeanne Whittome conduct their own love affair with the place, and it shows. The jumble of atmospheric public rooms, centuries old – wooden floors and chairs, antiques, rugs and pictures – exude a real warmth, and visitors are likely to rub shoulders with locals who patently adore the place. Paul's aim is to turn The Hoste into 'England's most popular inn.' Not too popular we hope: some things are best kept secret.

The Phew! factor

Gorgeous country town
meets gorgeous country inn.
A prize-winning combo.

Desirable Distractions An area of Outstanding Natural Beauty, boasting magnificent sand-duned beaches, bird sanctuaries, working windmills, old churches and antique shops. Build a day around historic estates such as Holkham and Sandringham, or golf at the Royal West Norfolk.

Love Bites Three air conditioned dining rooms provide varied and generous cuisine, with delightful service. As it's so close to the coast, they make a virtue of seafood. How does half a dozen Burnham Creek oysters on crushed ice with red wine and shallot vinegar sound? Remember, the mollusc is supposed to be an aphrodisiac.

Pillow Talk Jeanne has designed and refurbished the 35 well appointed rooms in various styles, some with four-poster beds and double baths. Centuries ago, intimacies of another sort took place here: the building was home to ladies of the night.

Getting There The inn is 45 minutes from Norwich. Take the A140 to Cromer and follow it to Burnham Market.

Maison Talbooth

Stratford Road, Dedham
Colchester, Essex CO7 6HN
tel: 01206 322367
fax: 01206 322752
maison@talbooth.co.uk
www.talbooth.com

Rooms and rates
10 rooms.
Double room for 2 people
per night including
continental breakfast and
VAT from £155 to £210

Proprietors
Gerald & Paul Milsom

A lovely tranquil air surrounds this former Victorian rectory, and no wonder: it's situated on a quiet bluff overlooking the Stour river valley whose green fields, undisturbed by buildings, stretch out to the medieval church at Stratford St Mary. Father and son proprietors Gerald and Paul Milsom have managed to create a perfect trinity with this plush country house, the more informal Milsom's hotel nearby, and Le Talbooth, their award-winning restaurant just down the road. The latter building even figures in one of John Constable's famous paintings.

The Phew! Factor

Spectacular views over Dedham Vale from many of the rooms, and river views from Le Talbooth.

Desirable Distractions This area has inspired great landscape artists – it might move you to set up an easel too. Otherwise hunt antiques in pretty villages nearby. In fine weather stroll along the River Stour, or go boating with a hotel picnic. Play croquet or giant chess in the grounds. Your move.

Love Bites Dinner is taken at the convivial waterside Le Talbooth, a short distance away. Tables await guests in a 16th century timber-framed dining room or pretty landscaped terrace beside the river – a real treat on balmy summer evenings. Their famous chateaubriand for two should set you up.

Pillow Talk No need to dress for breakfast here – it's served up in your room. The Shakespeare suite has a decadent sunken bath for two, so plunge in.

Getting There Maison Talbooth is easily reached from the M25, taking the A12 exit at Brentwood towards Ipswich. It lies 40 miles from London's Stansted airport.

The Norfolk Mead Hotel

Coltishall
Norwich NR12 7DN
tel: 01603 737531
fax: 01603 737521
info@norfolkmead.co.uk
www.norfolkmead.co.uk

Rooms and rates
10 rooms.
Double room for 2 people
per night including full
breakfast and VAT from
£80 to £140

Proprietors
Don & Jill Fleming

This exceptional Georgian manor house, with its rich period furnishings, traditional hospitality and fine food and wines, wins many hearts. Hosts Don and Jill Fleming have created a charming ambience set in lovely grounds running down to the meandering River Bure, close to the reedy marshes of the Norfolk Broads. This haven of East Anglian elegance is only a stallholder's pitch from Norwich with its castle, cobbled streets and covered markets. Lovers of the good life will find it here in abundance. This is tranquillity itself.

The Phew! factor

The perfect antidote to real life, with masses of Norfolk fresh air.

Desirable Distractions Champagne and strawberries in a rowing boat! A walled garden with double hammocks to swing in. The Broads and their teeming bird life. Bicycles to beetle about country lanes on, and gorgeous walks. (No wonder HRH loves life at Norfolk's Sandringham!)

Love Bites Log fires with pre-dinner drinks in winter. Candlelit meals from an ever-changing menu created by award-winning chefs. Fresh fish from the North Sea, game from the local estates, vegetables from the hotel gardens: you should be sated well before you've seen the wine list!

Pillow Talk Rooms are individually furnished: styles range from English country house to a suite of gorgeous Edwardian splendour with a huge antique brass bed and river views. And after the night before, pamper yourselves with luxurious toiletries or a little help from the resident beauty therapist.

Getting There Approaching Norwich, take the B1150 ring road exit. Turn right towards Wroxham after six miles, and travel a further 600 yards down this road.

The Pier at Harwich

The Quay, Harwich
Essex CO12 3HH
tel: 01255 241212
fax: 01255 551922
reception@pieratharwich.co.uk
www.pieratharwich.com

Rooms and rates
14 rooms.
Double room for 2 people
per night including
continental breakfast and
VAT from £80 to £150

Proprietors
Gerald & Paul Milsom

This hotel, two listed buildings combined, rests bang on the quayside of Harwich's historic port, where packet ships once set sail for Europe. Many rooms have commanding views of today's commercial bustle but within The Pier itself all is calm and charm. Landlubbers will like the restful sand, sea and stone colours of the decorative scheme, heightened by nautical accents. Public rooms have a pleasing buzz (perfect for the two of you to splice the mainbrace perhaps). Senior and junior ranks among the staff have evidently been signed up for good service.

The Phew! factor

This is a great seafarers' town, so take a deep breath of the briny and watch yachts, cargo ships and cruise liners chug by.

Desirable Distractions A bracing walk along the harbour and beach should be followed by a mooch into Harwich, birthplace of Captain Jones, who sailed the Mayflower to the new world. Clamber around the Redoubt Fort, the old lighthouses and lightships; or cosy up in the back row of the Electric Palace Cinema.

Love Bites This is the place to try the region's world-famous oysters. The Pier's prize-winning Harbourside restaurant and informal Ha'Penny Bistro specialise in seafood: no wonder, the chef catches it fresh each day at the quayside.

Pillow Talk The spacious Mayflower suite with its comfy king-size bed has a bird's-eye view over the estuary, but if that's not enough, there's also a telescope to keep you amused.

Getting There Harwich is reached by road via the A120 and is within easy walking distance of the mainline train station. The Pier Hotel is also accessible by boat.

Strattons

4 Ash Close, Swaffham
Norfolk PE37 7NH
tel: 01760 723845
fax: 01760 720458
enquiries@strattons-hotel.co.uk
www.strattons-hotel.co.uk

Rooms and rates
9 rooms.
Double room for 2 people
per night including
breakfast and VAT from
£100 to £170

Proprietors
Les & Vanessa Scott

Les and Vanessa Scott's Palladian villa, in a quiet corner of this Norfolk market town, is like an Aladdin's cave. Walls dazzle in cobalt blue, salmon pink and deep reds, accented with murals and ornaments. Furnishings are swathed in thick damasks and raw silks; an eclectic mélange of antiques, sculptures and objets d'art add to the mood. It might have gone over the top but the exuberance and theatricality of the decor gives the place tremendous oomph... The owners' love for their little treasure is palpable, and their 'green' commitment has justly brought many tourism awards.

The Phew! factor

The Venetian Room's bathroom has a mural of Botticelli's Venus: she's rising from the waves but you can just float serenely.

Desirable Distractions Breckland's forests, footpaths and heath encourage walking, riding or cycling. You can trot through 25 miles of track without meeting any roads. Strattons provides a picnic hamper to ease the exertions.

Love Bites Norfolk's well deserved Restaurant of the Year. The intense flavours of the organic produce and the heady atmosphere of the dining room conspire to make guests feel like 18th century voluptuaries. How about basil-scented pannacotta with smoked trout terrine or cauliflower crème caramel followed by thyme and lime sorbet?

Pillow Talk Try the flamboyantly decorated suite on two floors: a king-size bed flanked by doric columns with a large bath at its foot, and a ceiling painted with cherubs. Or the Red Room's four-poster (once slept in by Emma Hamilton) with its decadent embroideries and art.

Getting There From the M11 take the A10 and then the A11 to the A1065, turning left on to Swaffham Road and then right to Strattons.

Amberley Castle

Amberley, Nr Arundel
West Sussex BN18 9ND
tel: 01798 831992
fax: 01798 831998
info@amberleycastle.co.uk
www.amberleycastle.co.uk

Rooms and rates
19 rooms including 6 suites.
Double room for 2 people
per night including VAT from
£145 to £325

Proprietors
Martin & Joy Cummings

Imagine mighty 60 foot walls, flagstone floors, massive oak doors, mullioned windows and a two tonne portcullis: medieval Amberley Castle really is a corker. Owners Martin and Joy Cummings have harnessed 900 years of splendour with extraordinary style – room after room oozes a historical atmosphere that's softened by luxurious comforts. The setting – in the lee of the South Downs – adds to the magic, with pastoral views of vast manicured lawns and flower-filled gardens. At night the battlements are floodlit. Today's knights and damsels will be completely conquered.

The Phew! Factor

Readers of a leading national paper voted Amberley as having 'the world's most romantic bedrooms.' Sweet dreams.

Desirable Distractions Lovers should head for the lake, where on a tiny island they can swing in a hammock and gaze back at the Castle while the resident black swans glide by. There's croquet in the dry moat, a brand new 18-hole putting course and plenty of historic landmarks nearby.

Love Bites The 12th century Queens Room has a stunning barrel-vaulted ceiling and classical mural. The most romantic spot is Table eight, raised on a dais beside mullioned windows. Chef James Peyton's French inspired menu demands attention too, and the wine list is superb.

Pillow Talk Gorgeous bedrooms include Pevensey and Herstmonceux, with private access to the battlements; Chichester, whose double jacuzzi overlooks the castle walls; Amberley, with a six-foot carved four-poster and 'his and hers' bathrooms; and The Bishopric, converted from 17th century barns, where one suite contains a three-poster!

Getting There Amberley Castle is on the B2139, off the A29 between Bury and Storrington.

Bolebroke Mill

Edenbridge Road, Hartfield
East Sussex TN7 4JP
tel: 01892 770425
fax: 01892 770425
bolebrokemill@btinternet.com
www.bolebrokemillhotel.co.uk

Rooms and rates
5 rooms.
Double room for 2 people
per night including
breakfast (no VAT) from
£68 to £79

Proprietor
David Cooper

Bolebroke Mill, acclaimed as 'Fairy Story Hotel of the Year' and ranked number one by the *Observer* in its World's Most Romantic Hotels list, enjoys rustic seclusion at the end of a winding track, in pretty woodland with rippling mill streams and open meadows. Three Grade Two listed buildings – the ancient Watermill, the Elizabethan Miller's Barn and the Tudor Mill House – have been adapted to create an idyllic setting. The heavily beamed Millers' Barn is a particular pièce de résistance. Fairy tale indeed! This place is as dreamy as you'll find.

The Phew! factor

The Great Bed of Bolebroke has seen 600 years of history – the mattress is a lot newer!

Desirable Distractions The ancient machinery in the Mill House warrants inspection. Further afield you'll find more bricks oozing history: Anne Boleyn's Hever Castle; Rudyard Kipling's Batemans; Churchill's Chartwell; and Sissinghurst, with its glorious gardens.

Love Bites The imaginative morning banquets (acclaimed as the 'Best Breakfast in Britain') are the perfect prelude to the day. As Bolebroke has no restaurant, further satiating is provided at some good gastro haunts nearby.

Pillow Talk Rustic character is cleverly combined with contemporary comforts. Masses of country charm: four-poster beds, floral prints, squidgy sofas, walls bedecked with items of agricultural interest, country prints and watercolours, and ensuite bathrooms – two of which are idiosyncratically built into former corn storage bins.

Getting There From the M25 or A25, take the B2026 towards Tunbridge Wells and turn right past Perryhill Nursery on to an unmade road, then take the first right.

Chilston Park

Sandway, Lenham
Kent ME17 2BE
tel: 01622 859803
fax: 01622 858588
info@chilstonparkhotel.co.uk
www.chilstonparkhotel.co.uk

Rooms and rates
53 rooms including 4 suites.
Double room for 2 people
per night including full
breakfast and VAT from
£140.90 to £320.90

General Manager
Mike Rothwell

This Grade One listed 17th century mansion looks undeniably imposing, set as it is within 250 idyllic acres of lush Kent countryside with lake and verdant woodlands. The grand air is underlined in a series of tall reception rooms that nod decoratively towards rococo and classicism, which are filled with impressive antiques, family portraits, Persian rugs and objets d'art. It's impressive but welcoming: stuffiness is strictly reserved for sofas and winged armchairs by the fire. Friendly staff dance attendance, and at night hundreds of candles lend a truly theatrical air.

The Phew! Factor

A mesmerising golden glow from the flicker of hundreds of candles, lit nightly.

Desirable Distractions Choose from gentle strolls, croquet, tennis and snooker. Pick from a collection of castles: Hever, Leeds and Dover. Find green fingers at Sissinghurst, or sample a vintage or two at Lamberhurst Vineyards.

Love Bites Six dining rooms overlook lake and gardens. Most impressive is the Marble Hall, with its collection of gilt framed oil paintings glinting under candlelight – a gorgeous setting in which to enjoy award-winning cuisine and fine wines.

Pillow Talk Luxuriously appointed rooms, most with lake or parkland views, include 12 four-posters. Room numbers are dispensed with in favour of names reflecting themes such as Gothic, Art Deco, Raj and Camelot. Today's Arthur and Guinevere should find their heart's desire in the latter!

Getting There From London head towards Maidstone on the M20 (or join at Junction 3 of the M25). Take the A20 towards Ashford at Junction 8 and follow signs to Lenham.

Howard's House

Teffont Evias, Salisbury
Wiltshire SP3 5RJ
tel: 01722 716392
fax: 01722 716820
enq@howardshousehotel.com
www.howardshousehotel.com

Rooms and rates
9 suites.
Double room for 2 people
per night including full
breakfast and VAT from
£135 to £155

Proprietor
Bill Thompson

Built in 1623 and acquired by Christopher Mayne in 1692, Howard's House stands in virtually unchanged rural surroundings just outside the Wiltshire village of Teffont, where Mayne's direct descendant is still lord of the manor. Pretty gardens with ancient box hedges, rolling lawns and secret corners are suffused with the scent of jasmine and cottage flowers: a quintessential English hideaway. Original stone plaques of Charles I and the Lion of England hint at royal affiliations. Mind all the cool elegance doesn't go to your head!

The Phew! factor

Enthrone yourself in Room Seven: a loo with the best view anywhere! (Would you believe it?)

Desirable Distractions After blissful nights come ancient rites. Stonehenge is a stone's throw distant. Old Sarum, Salisbury Cathedral and Wilton House are equally close. Splendid walks abound, and country pursuits can be arranged. Quieter pastimes include croquet on the lawn.

Love Bites The freshest home grown ingredients. Dinner menus include acclaimed favourites such as loin of smoked venison with braised cabbage and bacon, foie gras, truffle pithivier and a blackcurrant sauce – all accompanied by fine wines. Breakfast is an equally grand affair.

Pillow Talk Floral prints and restful pastels in the nine luxurious bedrooms – some with four-poster beds – highlight the relaxed ambience of Howard's House. Bathrooms are furnished with cotton bathrobes and other creature comforts. Haven't slept better, said a recent guest.

Getting There Turn left off the A303, two miles after the A36 Wylye intersection. Head for the B3089. Turn right after 1/3 mile and the hotel is 400 yards on the right.

Le Poussin at Parkhill

Beaulieu Road, Lyndhurst
Hampshire SO43 7FZ
tel: 02380 282944
fax: 02380 283268
sales@lepoussinatparkhill.co.uk
www.lepoussin.co.uk

Rooms and rates
18 rooms including 4 suites.
Double room for 2 people
per night including buffet
breakfast and VAT from
£110 to £240

Proprietors
Alex & Caroline Aitken

Proprietors Alex and Caroline Aitken know how to cook. And how: they have notched up a Michelin star, AA rosettes, Egon Ronay's plaudits and various national newspaper 'Restaurant of the Year' awards. But their self-styled New Forest restaurant with accommodation by no means suggests that staying over at Le Poussin should be simply an afterthought. This is a gorgeous Georgian house with rich historical connections, decorated in period style in an elevated countryside position. The welcoming atmosphere and polished French service here are a treat.

The Phew! factor

The place to be when taste buds hanker for sublime cuisine.

Desirable Distractions A leisurely stroll around the house's 12 acres of picturesque parkland will satiate guests simply wanting an after-dinner stroll. Private access leading to the New Forest is a nice appetiser for the sandy beaches and boating life further afield.

Love Bites Alex's acclaimed cuisine is the quintessence of great taste. You'll surely ooh and aah over terrine of roast poussin, foie gras and prunes followed by turbot with wild mushrooms (possibly picked by Caroline that morning) rounded off, appropriately, with hot passion fruit soufflé.

Pillow Talk 14 elegantly furnished rooms are located in the main building, another four in a separate coach house. Perhaps opt for the Gardener's Cottage with its own private walled garden? Or – in some rooms – slide between the sheets in a French sleigh bed.

Getting There Take the M3/M27/M271 to Southampton and join the A35 to Lyndhurst. The house is on the B3056, a mile and a half south-east of the town.

Priory Bay

Priory Drive, Seaview
Isle of Wight   PO34 5BU
tel: 01983 613146
fax: 01983 616539
enquiries@priorybay.co.uk
www.priorybay.co.uk

Rooms and rates
18 rooms and 9 cottages.
Double room for 2 people
per night including full
breakfast and VAT from
£120 to £260

Proprietor
Andrew Palmer

This country house hotel by the sea was once a medieval priory, next a Tudor farmhouse, and then home to Georgian gentry. Visible evidence of these eras piles one layer of charm upon the other – quite aside from its commanding position overlooking the Solent, surrounded by 70 idyllic acres including its own private beach. Sympathetic restoration has produced eclectic and tastefully furnished rooms with plump sofas and large sash windows (including an unusual octagonal one over an Elizabethan fireplace). Rather like the island itself, the atmosphere here is friendly and laid back.

The Phew! factor

Corner of the Isle of Wight where everything's very much all right.

Desirable Distractions Direct access to the private golden sands and rock pools of Priory Bay would in itself satisfy most romantics, but the grounds also offer an outdoor pool, nine-hole golf course, tennis courts and woodlands. Get the wind in your hair with great sailing and watersports.

Love Bites Diners can feast splendidly from a modern European menu against a backdrop of giant murals of the island long ago. The pretty terrace is a draw in good weather, and you can claw your way through juicy lobsters at the Seafood Café nested in the woods above the bay.

Pillow Talk Choose between rooms in the main building – decorated in dreamy pastels, some with sea views – and those in the cottages, some thatched. Each offers individual charms, such as a snug double bed up in the eaves. Very appealing.

Getting There Take the ferry to Fishbourne from Portsmouth. Join the A3055 to Sandown. Turn left on to the B3330 for Bembridge and then left towards Seaview.

London

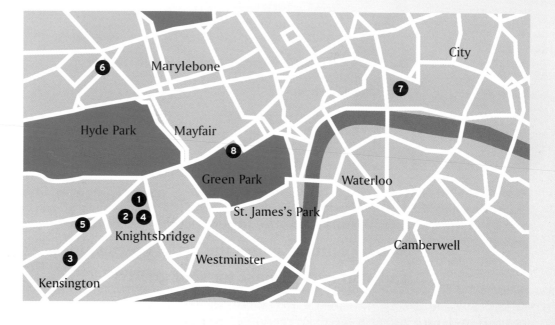

Marylebone

City

6

7

Hyde Park

Mayfair

8

Green Park

Waterloo

1

St. James's Park

2 4

5

Knightsbridge

Camberwell

3

Westminster

Kensington

Room for Romance

Why we love London

Steeped in history, it's been the scene of countless seductions

Up-for-it lovers can party till dawn in the world's most happening nightspots

Whatever you love best, you'll find it here

"If all the world and love were young,
And truth in every shepherd's tongue,
These pretty pleasures might me move
To live with thee, and be thy love."

Walter Raleigh

Blakes

33 Roland Gardens
South Kensington
London SW7 3PF
tel: 020 7370 6701
fax: 020 7373 0442
blakes@easynet.co.uk
www.blakeshotels.com

Rooms and rates
52 rooms, including 9 suites.
Double room for 2 people
per night including VAT from
£300 to £400

Proprietor
Anouska Hempel

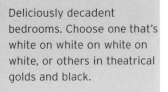

Visually dazzling Blakes – owned and opened by Anouska Hempel in the heart of Kensington – is one of London's plum designer hotels. Each of its 52 rooms is decorated in a uniquely original, vivid and dramatic way. Witness the sensuous colour schemes: black and mustard; a palette of cardinal reds; lavender, vanilla and rich tea rose. This sought-after place is recognised by the cognoscenti as a true 'couture' hotel with a spirit that doesn't ignore 21st century needs. 'Fabulousness personified,' enthused a recent guest. It's hard to argue.

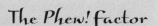
The Phew! Factor

Deliciously decadent bedrooms. Choose one that's white on white on white on white, or others in theatrical golds and black.

Desirable Distractions The central London location means it's minutes from glossy Knightsbridge and Chelsea stores, and some of the great museums. Lose yourself (metaphorically speaking) in the hotel's tiny evergreen courtyard or hang out in the stylish bar.

Love Bites A leading food guide described the dining room as 'like an opium den managed by Coco Chanel.' It is certainly heady and intoxicating. The East/West fusion cuisine is beautifully presented. Wines from the excellent list are best imbibed then dabbed behind the ears.

Pillow Talk And so to bed – but which? Atmospheric bedrooms let you choose between the inscrutable pleasures of the Orient; snuggling up à deux in a Loire château; being swept away on a 30s cruise liner or hiding in a sultan's harem.

Getting There Blakes is easily reached from the M4, sitting between Old Brompton Road and Fulham Road. Nearest tube station: South Kensington.

The Capital

Th[e] ...

34-36 S...
Londor ...
tel: 02...
fax: 02...
PAVILI(...
www.m...

Rooms ...
30 roor...
Double ...
per nig...
contine ...
VAT fro...

Propri...
Danny ...

22-24 Basil Street, Knightsbridge
London   SW3 1AT
tel: 020 7589 5171
fax: 020 7225 0011
reservations@capitalhotel.co.uk
www.capitalhotel.co.uk

Rooms and rates
48 rooms including 8 suites.
Double room for 2 people
per night including full
breakfast and VAT from
£292 to £475

Proprietor
David Levin

At first ...
townh(...
decora...
beyonc...
kaleidc...
you fii...
in the ...
crash ...
film ar...
house ...
'We dc...

The Capital is one of London's few notable family-run hotels, and very much the creation of its Scottish proprietor, David Levin. His good taste is indelibly stamped on this fine establishment where much – such as interior decoration and furniture – has been privately commissioned from the likes of Nina Campbell and David Linley. The result melds the exquisite with the plush; the whole oozes a rich understated chic. The Capital is nothing if not discreet, as witnessed by the patronage of royalty, heads of state and leading celebrities.

Desirable Distractions You're slap bang in smartest Knightsbridge, which means the shopping cannot be beaten. Three royal parks are within strolling distance, while the West End is a mere cab ride away. Either way the best of London lies at your feet.

Love Bites Eating here is a sublime experience: both menu and wine list have been justly lauded, with chef Eric Chavot's outstanding French-inspired cuisine recently winning its second Michelin star. The room, with its central chandelier, looks ravishing, and service is exemplary.

Pillow Talk Each room has been individually and richly designed; mattresses are all hand-made and some beds are swathed with magnificent canopies. Marble bathrooms have generous baths, powerful showers and high quality toiletries, plus fluffy towels and bathrobes. The pampering here is patently carried to perfection.

Getting There The hotel is ten minutes from both the M4 and the West End. Nearest tube station: Knightsbridge.

The Phew! factor

A leading food critic calls The Capital's restaurant 'as good a place as you can eat in London.'

Th

8-10 Que
London
tel: 020
fax: 020
gallery@
www.eeh

Rooms a
36 rooms
Double r
per night
breakfas
£141 to £

General
Mukul Bi

The Vict
pheric s
contemp
where i
plumbin
otherwi
furnitur
oriental
Morris,
table. It
day enjc

92

Index to hotels

● Members of Pride of Britain Hotels

Three ways to say "I love you"

Special occasions call for special gifts. Whether you're celebrating an engagement, an anniversary, the birth of a child, or just the fact that you're in love, a diamond will illuminate the day with a special magic. For over 3,000 years, men and women have known that a diamond is the most dazzling way to show your love. Diamonds are radiant. They're rare. They're an enduring symbol of passion and commitment.

• • •

From classic pieces of jewellery to works of art on the cutting edge of fashion, there's a diamond piece to suit every taste. Whether you're after a simple solitaire or something more dramatic, diamonds will enhance your unique look. But if you're following the lead of style icons like Sharon Stone, Uma Thurman and Sarah Jessica Parker, then the Trilogy design is for you. Since the fashion world discovered it two years ago, the three-stone diamond ring has graced the fingers of the famous, including Madonna and Sadie Frost... but with the launch of the trilogy pendant, we'll see it adorning celebrity décolletages, too.

• • •

An intimate getaway is the perfect time to look back on other special times you've spent together, reaffirm your commitment to a happy and loving future, and just relish adoring each other so much, right now! And there's no better way to inspire romance than to lavish a little luxury on your partner, with a combination of flowers, perfectly-prepared food, champagne, irresistibly crisp white sheets, and the gift of a precious piece of jewellery to make sure the evening is truly unforgettable.

• • •

So go on... spoil her, seduce her, make a statement you'll never forget. All it takes is a present that also symbolises your past and your future: a ring that says "I love you" – three times over.

the
tr:logy
designer diamond collection

www.forevermark.com

Win
a luxury weekend for two at Stapleford Park

Here's an opportunity not to be missed! We are delighted to offer one lucky couple the chance to win a fabulous free weekend for two worth more than £800 at Stapleford Park, the luxurious hotel and sporting estate in the heart of Leicestershire. To be taken during 2003 (dates are subject to availability), this superb prize will include two nights' accommodation with both dinner and breakfast, plus a bottle of champagne in your room, at what is unquestionably one of England's finest stately homes.

To enter this great prize draw, visit our website at *www.room4romance.com* You can read more about Stapleford Park on page 48.

Hotel of the Year 2003

Which of the fabulous places featured in these pages is the ultimate romantic destination? Let us have your views and your votes, and you could win a case of superb Perrier-Jouët champagne.

Send us your nominations for the **Room for Romance Hotel of the Year 2003**, together with the reasons for your choice. Details of the winning hotel will be announced in the press and on our website (**www.room4romance.com**) in time for Valentine's Day 2003, so nominations should reach us no later than 10 January. You'll find a voting form on our website. Alternatively, you can complete and cut out the reply form below and send it to us at the address shown.

Our case of champagne will be awarded to the sender of the best, most original or entertaining reason for nominating the winning hotel.

My vote for the **Room for Romance Hotel of the Year 2003** goes to: _____

Because _____
_____
_____
_____

Dates of my visit _____

Name _____
Address _____
_____
Tel _____
Email _____

I confirm that this nomination is made independently and understand that votes from relatives or friends of the owners, managers or staff of the property nominated are not eligible.

Signed _____ Date _____

This reply form should be posted before 10 January 2003 to:
Room for Romance Hotel of the Year 2003
Freeway Media Ltd, 4 Ravey Street, London EC2A 4XX.

Useful contacts

Visitor information:
British Isles and Ireland

Cumbria	015394 44444
	www.gocumbria.co.uk
East of England	01473 822922
	www.visitbritain.com
Guernsey	01481 726611
	www.guernseytouristboard.com
Heart of England	01905 761100
	www.visitheartofengland.com
Ireland	0800 039 7000 (UK)
	+353 (1) 602 4000 (Dublin)
	www.ireland.travel.ie
Jersey	01534 500700
	www.jersey.com
London	020 7932 2017
	www.londontouristboard.com
Northern Ireland	02890 321221
	www.nitourism.com
Northumbria	0191 375 3004
	www.visitnorthumbria.com
North West	01942 821222
	www.visitnorthwest.com
Scotland	0131 332 2433
	www.visitscotland.com
South East England	01892 500315
	www.southeastengland.uk.com
Southern England	02380 625400
	www.visitsouthernengland.com
Wales	029 2049 9909
	www.visitwales.com
Yorkshire	01904 707961
	www.yorkshirevisitor.com

Rail operators:

National Rail Inquiries	0845 748 4950
	www.nationalrail.co.uk
First Great Western	01793 499400
	www.greatwesterntrains.co.uk
GNER	01904 523072
	www.gner.co.uk
Midland Mainline	08457 125678
	www.midlandmainline.com
Scotrail	0345 484950
	www.scotrail.co.uk
South West Trains	0845 6000 650
	www.southwesttrains.co.uk
Virgin Trains	0870 789 1111
	www.virgin.com/trains

Motoring organisations:

AA	0990 500600
	www.theaa.com
RAC	020 8917 2747
	www.rac.co.uk

Room for Romance

Freeway Media Ltd, 4 Ravey Street, London EC2A 4XX
T +44 (0)20 7739 1434   **F** +44 (0)20 7739 1424
info@room4romance.com   www.room4romance.com